Thou hast but two rare cabinets full of treasure,

    The *Trinitie* and *Incarnation:*

      Thou hast unlockt them both,

    And made them jewels to betroth

      The work of thy creation

Unto thy self in everlasting pleasure.

                George Herbert, "Ungratefulnesse"

Jesus Christ and the Life of the Mind

MARK A. NOLL

WILLIAM B. EERDMANS PUBLISHING COMPANY

GRAND RAPIDS, MICHIGAN / CAMBRIDGE, U.K.

Published 2011 by

Wm. B. Eerdmans Publishing Co.

2140 Oak Industrial Drive N.E., Grand Rapids, Michigan 49505 /
P.O. Box 163, Cambridge CB3 9PU U.K.

www.eerdmans.com

Printed in the United States of America

17 16 15 14 13 12 11   7 6 5 4 3 2 1

Library of Congress Cataloging-in-Publication Data

Noll, Mark A., 1946-
Jesus Christ and the life of the mind / Mark A. Noll.
p.   cm.
Includes index.
ISBN 978-0-8028-6637-0 (cloth: alk. paper)
1. Jesus Christ — Person and offices.
2. Learning and scholarship — Religious aspects — Christianity.
I. Title.

BT205.N65   2011
232′.8 — dc22

2011005879

The hymn stanza by Carl Daw on page 39 is used by permission of Hope Publishing Company. Words: Carl P. Daw, Jr. © 1988 Hope Publishing Company,
Carol Stream, IL 60188. All rights reserved. Used by permission. Reprinted under license #65984

Except where noted, Scripture is taken from the HOLY BIBLE, NEW INTERNA-
TIONAL VERSION. Copyright 1973, 1978, 1984 International Bible Society.
Used by permission of Zondervan Bible Publishers.

To

Jon Pott

Contents

—⁓⁓—

Introduction

———⦿⦿⦿———

C hristianity is defined by the person and work of Jesus Christ. The doctrinal truths supporting this assertion — as set out in Scripture and summarized in the major Christian creeds — provide a compelling reason for pursuing human learning. At the same time, they also offer strong protection against the abuses of human learning. Understanding more about Christ and his work not only opens a wide doorway to learning, but also checks tendencies toward idolatry that are as potent among scholars as in the rest of humankind.

The person of Christ and the work of Christ must, however, be considered in the fullness of Christian faith. The Trinity — Father, Son, and Spirit in the unity of the Godhead — provides the essential, if also deeply mysterious, starting point. Other aspects of Christian faith also play a part in human learning: for example, the divine creation of the world, the fact of human sinfulness, God's merciful resolve to rescue sinners, the convicting work of the Holy Spirit, and the providential oversight of everything that ever takes place. Yet intrinsic to all such Christian realities are the person of Christ and the meaning of his work for all humanity in all human history. To understand that person and to fathom that work is to approach the center of Christianity itself.

My contention in this book is that coming to know Christ provides the most basic possible motive for pursuing the tasks of human learning.

In the chapters that follow the truly essential points come from the general storehouse of classical doctrine that has been appropriated by believers in all the Christian traditions. Yet it is also inevitable that, since I have experienced the Christian faith personally as an evangelical Protestant, my understanding of Christ and his work will be colored by evangelical experiences and convictions. The book's evangelical provenance will also be evident by the fact that it extends some of the arguments I first published in *The Scandal of the Evangelical Mind*.[1] The message in this book for my fellow evangelicals can be put simply: if what we claim about Jesus Christ is true, then evangelicals should be among the most active, most serious, and most open-minded advocates of general human learning. Evangelical hesitation about scholarship in general or about pursuing learning wholeheartedly is, in other words, antithetical to the Christ-centered basis of evangelical faith.

Yet, if there is an evangelical coloring to the book, and if evangelicals are the ones addressed most directly, I also hope that Catholics, Orthodox, other kinds of Protestants, and representatives of the world's proliferating indigenous churches will find encouragement for approaching human learning as a distinctly Christian enterprise. In addition, I hope that nonbelievers and believers adhering to other faiths may find some clues in these pages for why at least some Christian supernaturalists are wholeheartedly committed to the tasks of learning.

The book is divided into chapters outlining a Christ-centered framework for learning, followed by chapters trying to show how that framework might be put to use. The first chapter offers a sketch from the Bible of main assertions about the person and work of Jesus Christ and then suggests how this diffuse biblical teaching was sharply focused in the great early creeds that summarized so capably the essential ingredients of Christian faith. The point of this exercise is to assert that orthodox Christology (= doctrine about Christ and his

1. *The Scandal of the Evangelical Mind* (Grand Rapids: Eerdmans, 1994).

work) provides an ideal place to stand from which to view the vast domains of human learning.

The book's second chapter describes a catalogue of christological encouragements to study. The intent is to show that traditional teaching about Jesus provides many powerful motivations for serious scholarship. In the third chapter I move beyond general encouragements to specific suggestions for how the Christology of the classic creeds might guide scholarship. It describes several stances toward learning, or expectations about the shape of scholarly results, that flow directly from this source. They are labeled as doubleness, contingency, particularity, and self-denial.

Then in chapters 4 through 7 I try to get specific. The goal of the fourth chapter is to show how a traditionally evangelical view of Christ's substitutionary atonement for sinners offers pointers for scholarship on many issues and at many levels. The next three chapters are discipline-specific in thinking about how christological realities might ground specific study in history, science, and biblical study itself.

For all the arguments attempted in this book, I am acutely aware of my amateur status and of many mistakes I am bound to make. But especially in chapters 4 through 7, where there is pontification on a number of highly complex academic issues, I hope readers will benefit as much from encouragement to think carefully about the areas of their own expertise as from my inevitably partial grasp of particular problems in particular disciplines.

The book's postscript returns to issues treated at greater length in *The Scandal of the Evangelical Mind.* It offers an updated assessment of the circumstances and possibilities for human learning in the American evangelical world and allows me to revisit questions of historical development, where I feel most at home, in order to answer the question, how fares "the evangelical mind" today?

Some of the material in the book has been published in earlier form, though everything has been reconsidered and rewritten for this volume. In addition, since the publication of *The Scandal of the Evangelical Mind,* I have been privileged to address related issues in seminars, classes, and lectures before a number of academic, church, and parachurch audiences. The opportunity to make these presentations has left me grateful beyond words for many useful suggestions, helpful criticisms, and heartfelt accounts of others' academic experiences. A guide to further reading, where at least some intellectual influences are indicated, and a closing set of acknowledgments, where more personal debts are discharged, round off the book.

*   *   *

The Gospel of John ends with words that are altogether fitting for the conclusion of that matchless account of Jesus the Messiah. Almost incidentally, the words also touch the concerns of scholarship, for they refer to the realm of words, where all aspiring scholars find a true home: "Jesus did many other things as well. If every one of them were written down, I suppose that even the whole world would not have room for the books that would be written" (21:25). What is true for the life and work of Christ in general is also true for the life of the mind. If the meaning of what Jesus did and is exceeds the capacity of all the books that could be written, so too the meaning of what Jesus did and is, with respect only to the intellectual life, exceeds the capacity of all the books that could ever be written. Christian believers who realize that it is impossible ever to fathom the depths of wisdom and knowledge hidden in Jesus Christ nonetheless know that the proper place to begin serious intellectual labor is the same place where we begin all other serious human enterprises. That place is the heart of our religion, which is the revelation of God in Jesus Christ.

ONE

A Place to Stand . . . from Which to See

———❧❧❧———

A lthough the various forms of traditional Christianity present
sometimes strikingly different versions of the faith, they also
share a common inheritance in the foundational theology of the classical Christian creeds. Christian bodies that claim to follow "no creed
but the Bible" put themselves at an enormous disadvantage for many
purposes, not least for promoting Christian learning, because they
cut themselves off from the vitally important work that has been accomplished by the numberless assemblies making up the communion of saints. That communion stretching back in time to the apostolic age and out in space to the ends of the earth is crucial for
grasping the meaning of divine revelation in itself and for understanding how that revelation illuminates the world as a whole.

An unusually important place in Christian history has been oc-
cupied by the saints who lived during the fourth and fifth centuries
A.D., that is, during the era when Christianity moved from being an il-
legal and culturally despised sect to becoming a formally recognized
religion of the Roman Empire. Their challenge, in what might be
called the church's first intellectual breathing space, was to summarize the faith in authoritative short statements that could specify what
Christianity was, define a curriculum for new converts, provide formulas for use in worship, and build barriers against false teaching.

The prime defining statements that resulted — especially the Apostles' Creed, the so-called Nicene Creed, and the Chalcedonian definition of Christ's divine-human unity — all functioned as key resources for meeting those needs. Yet beyond their historic value for worship, proclamation, catechesis, and theology, the creeds offered — and continue to offer — precisely what is needed as a grounding for Christian learning. They do so because they represent the distillation of concentrated reflection on Scripture and of hard-won wisdom time-tested by Christian experience.

The ancient creeds became authoritative in the early centuries because they were thoroughly, profoundly, comprehensively, and passionately rooted in Scripture. They retain their importance only because they remain such forceful summaries of biblical revelation. Yet because the creeds also represented the most intense effort imaginable to root the biblical realities of Jesus Christ in the reigning thought forms of the fourth and fifth centuries, they remain important for later eras because they were such superlative exercises in Christian thinking when they were first written. Perhaps most importantly, the creeds concentrate with fearsome energy on the themes that define the heart of Christianity. They remain important for Christian scholarship because they have stood the test of time as faithful summaries of biblical revelation concerning the person and work of Christ.

Examples of Biblical Revelation Summarized by the Creeds

As only the barest sample of the vast material summarized in the creeds, I would like to sketch two strands of that biblical teaching. The first concerns use of the term "glory" in both New and Old Testaments as a word describing the presence of God; the second treats images of Christ in the book of Revelation. Both strands display the diverse richness that made the Christian faith so compelling, but also so challenging, for those who summarized biblical teaching in succinct creedal statements.

Glory

In the Old Testament, God's glory was described as an ineffable splendor that displayed his holiness and marked him as distinct from the creatures; that glory also spoke of his true character that at the end of time would be manifest throughout all creation. In the story of the Israelites after the exodus from Egypt, the glory of God was an overwhelming and frightening presence: "To the Israelites the glory of the LORD looked like a consuming fire on top of the mountain" (Exod. 24:17). Later, at a time of worship, "Moses could not enter the Tent of Meeting because the cloud had settled upon it, and the glory of the LORD filled the tabernacle" (Exod. 40:35). This identification of God's glory as an awe-filled presence would continue long after Moses had left the scene, as was recorded once during the reign of King Solomon: "When the priests withdrew from the Holy Place, the cloud filled the temple of the LORD. And the priests could not perform their service because of the cloud, for the glory of the LORD filled his temple" (1 Kings 8:10-11). The fear-inspiring quality of the divine glory was reflected even in the New Testament when the shepherds in the hills above Bethlehem received a message from God on the night of Jesus' birth: "An angel of the Lord appeared to them, and the glory of the Lord shone around them, and they were terrified" (Luke 2:9).

The clearest explanation for why such holy dread attended the presence of God's glory was recorded during the life of Moses when he asked for an unusual gift: "Then Moses said [to the LORD], 'Now show me your glory.' And the LORD said, 'I will cause all my goodness to pass in front of you, and I will proclaim my name, the LORD, in your presence. I will have mercy on whom I will have mercy, and I will have compassion on whom I will have compassion. But,' he said, 'you cannot see my face, for no one may see me and live'" (Exod. 33:18-20). In this strand of Old Testament revelation, the glory of God was to be honored, revered, worshiped, but also feared — and from a safe distance.

Yet, as awesome as the glory of the Lord appeared to ancient Israel — terrifying as the face of God was — so too did Israel's prophets foresee a day when that divine glory would be manifest for all to see. To the prophet Ezekiel this revelation of divine glory was construed as a sign of apocalyptic judgment: "I will display my glory among the nations, and all the nations will see the punishment I inflict and the hand I lay upon them" (Ezek. 39:21). But to the prophet Habakkuk the connotation of this eschatological revealing was more hopeful:

> For the earth will be filled with the knowledge of the glory
> of the LORD,
> as the waters cover the sea.
>
> (Hab. 2:14)

Such prophetic words underscored the splendor of the divine presence, but they did not fundamentally alter the sense of God's unapproachable transcendence that was conveyed throughout the revelation to Israel.

The Hebrew term for glory *(kābôd)* that was used in these passages expressed a metaphorical sense of "weight" as "splendor, glory, or honor." In the Greek translation of the Old Testament (the Septuagint) and in the New Testament itself, the term became *doxa,* which means "brightness, splendor, and radiance" manifest as "glory, majesty, magnificence, splendor" and also "fame, renown, and honor."[1]

For the New Testament writers who proclaimed the "gospel" or "good news" about Jesus Christ, it was of highest importance that his presence and his work be described by this same word. Sometimes, to be sure, New Testament usage resembled what had been said in the Old Testament by pointing to an awesome eschatological future. So it was on the Mount of Transfiguration when Peter, James, and John received a glimpse of how the exalted Christ would one day appear: "Peter and his companions were very sleepy, but when they became fully awake, they saw his glory and the two men [Moses and Elijah] standing with him" (Luke 9:32). The Synoptic Gospels also record Jesus speaking of the end of the age in terms of his own awe-inspiring glory: "At that time they will see the Son of Man coming in a cloud with power and great glory" (Luke 21:27, with parallels in Matt. 24:30 and Mark 13:26).

---

1. W. F. Arndt and F. W. Gingrich, *A Greek-English Lexicon of the New Testament and Other Early Christian Literature* (Chicago: University of Chicago Press, 1957), on *doxa* and related words, 202-3.

But the revolutionary use of this term in the New Testament came not in its reference to the End, but in its application to the present appearance of Jesus Christ. What no one in ancient Israel could look upon and live was now being shown to all people as the gift of life itself. So it was in stories from Jesus' infancy, as when in the temple at Jerusalem the aged Simeon saw the young child and then praised God in these words:

> "My eyes have seen your salvation,
> > which you have prepared in the sight of all people,
> a light for revelation to the Gentiles
> > and for glory to your people Israel."
>
> > > > (Luke 2:30-32)

So it was in later recapitulations of the meaning of Christ's life and work, as in the opening words of the Epistle to the Hebrews: "In the past God spoke to our forefathers through the prophets . . . , but in these last days he has spoken to us by his Son. . . . The Son is the radiance of God's glory" (Heb. 1:1-3).

The Gospel of John offered the sharpest New Testament emphasis on Jesus as the one in whom the glory of God dwelt and who in his person opened that glory to all. A stunning announcement at the start of the Gospel asked hearers, in effect, to remember how God's glory had been experienced in ancient Israel so that they could understand the momentous thing that had happened in their midst: "The Word became flesh and made his dwelling among us. We have seen his glory, the glory of the One and Only, who came from the Father, full of grace and truth" (John 1:14). Elsewhere in his Gospel John underscored what it meant for the unapproachable holiness of God to become approachable in Jesus Christ. At the conclusion of his account of the marriage feast at Cana, where Jesus turned water into wine, John said of this incident, "He thus revealed his glory, and his disciples put their faith in him" (2:11). Later in the Gospel John interwove the theme of divine glory into his account of how Jesus raised Lazarus from the dead. When anxious friends of the dying Lazarus came seeking help for their friend, Jesus replied that the sickness of Lazarus was "for God's glory so that God's Son may be glorified through it." And then after Lazarus had been raised from the dead, Jesus said, "Did I not tell you that if you believed, you would see the glory of God?" (11:4, 40).

John's insistence that the divine glory was manifest in Jesus Christ distinguished his contribution to early Christian proclamation, but it was by no means unique. Thus, we find in Luke's account of Jesus' appearances after the resurrection a story of two dejected disciples who, on their way to Emmaus, encountered the risen Jesus, who asked them, "Did not the Christ have to suffer these things and then enter his glory?" (Luke 24:26). And when the apostle Paul was telling the Romans about the significance of Christian baptism, he too linked the rising of Jesus from the dead with the manifestation of divine splendor: "We were therefore buried with him through baptism into death in order that, just as Christ was raised from the dead through the glory of the Father, we too may live a new life" (Rom. 6:4).

The New Testament claim made by this full range of passages was audacious in the extreme: the one God of Israel — who had created the world, who had initiated a covenant with a distinct people through their father Abraham, who had then protected that people for the sake of his own name, but who also existed as a perfectly holy being in unapproachable glory — that God had entered human history in the person of Jesus Christ. Jesus, in turn, did not simply trail clouds of glory in the sense of a romantic metaphor, but he actually embodied the divine splendor in such a way that, as the First Epistle of John puts it, "we have heard . . . we have seen with our eyes . . . we have looked at and our hands have touched" (1 John 1:1).

Then, most remarkably, the New Testament records that the glory of the Lord, as revealed in Jesus Christ, could be communicated to those who followed him. The humble creature was being given that which belonged by rights exclusively to the Creator. In the Gospel of John once more, the Evangelist records a prayer that Jesus spoke immediately before his passion. One of its central elements was the desire of Jesus that the glory he shared with the Father would be communicated to those who followed him: Jesus "looked toward heaven and prayed: 'Father, the time has come. Glorify your Son, that your Son may glorify you. . . . And now, Father, glorify me in your presence with the glory I had with you before the world began. . . . I have given them [his disciples] the glory you gave me, that they may be one. . . . I want those you have given me to be with me where I am, and to see my glory" (John 17:1, 5, 22, 24). Even more expansively, the apostle Paul, in words addressed to the new believing community in Corinth, contrasted the glory of God that was revealed to Moses (from which people hid their faces) to the glory that believers in Christ enjoyed because of the work of the Holy Spirit. At the end of a lengthy comparison, the apostle summarized the full weight of the earlier revelation to Israel and its transformation by the revelation of God in Christ with another strong statement: "And we, who with unveiled faces all reflect the Lord's glory, are being transformed into his likeness with ever-increasing glory, which comes from the Lord, who is the Spirit" (2 Cor. 3:18).

In this range of passages from the Old and New Testaments concerning the glory of God, it is obvious that early Christian writers were making unusually bold claims about the person and work of Jesus Christ. He appears on earth and appears to be human, but he is also said to possess — and to bestow — the glory of the one true God. Mysteries, conundrums, paradoxes, and apparent contradictions abound in this strand of biblical revelation: How could an apparently ordinary human born to an apparently ordinary Galilean woman be said to partake of what the one true God enjoyed as his sole prerogative? If Jesus somehow did embody the divine glory, why was it recorded that he seemed to lack the prerogatives of deity — that he needed to eat and drink, that he became weary, that he professed not to know everything, and (most counterintuitively) that he could die? But maybe, if testimonies about the glory of God in Christ were true, then the reports of human limitations were deceptive and Jesus never *really* experienced the ordinary human weaknesses he only *seemed* to experience. Or perhaps Jesus was like ordinary humans in only part of his person while the rest was the habitation of God. Most disconcerting of all, the religion of ancient Israel was so militantly monotheistic, it seemed incredible that someone supposedly learned in the Hebrew Scriptures could ever imagine ascribing deity of any sort to a mere human being.

If such puzzles were not enough, it is important to remember that teaching about the glory of God represents only one of many trajectories in the biblical record that early believers perceived as leading from the first revelations to Israel toward full fruition in the revelation of God in Christ.

In the early centuries of the Christian church it was no easy matter to sort all this out, but sorting it out was precisely what the church faced as a community gathered to worship God-in-Christ, and also as a community of belief pressed to explain — to prospective converts, incredulous opponents, suspicious public officials — what it all meant. The main creedal statements represented the most important efforts to summarize what the early Christians knew they had experienced, but also knew they needed to formulate for themselves and for others as carefully as they could. Because these statements concentrated so hard on getting the Biggest Questions right about Christ and his work, they, in turn, became ideal guides for shedding the light of Christ on the worlds of learning.

The Lamb That Was Slain

As with a theme like the glory of God that stretches throughout Scripture, a parallel plentitude with similar depth is found in more compact parts of the Bible, like the book of Revelation that draws the New Testament to a close. In this strange book of visions, wonders, and the renewal of the earth, one of the most remarkable things is its diverse and complex depiction of Jesus. As with the biblical theme of divine glory, so in Revelation's picture of Christ, the early church was challenged to say succinctly what a tumultuous array of images, teachings, and descriptions might mean.

The book of Revelation's profusion of images describing Jesus Christ is nothing less than psychedelic. As only a partial list, he is pictured as:

the faithful witness (1:5)
the firstborn from the dead (1:5)

the ruler of the kings of the earth (1:5)
someone "like a son of man" (1:13)
the First and the Last, who died and came to life again (2:8)
the Son of God, whose eyes are like blazing fire and whose feet
    are like burnished bronze (2:18)
the one who searches hearts and minds (2:23)
the Amen, the faithful and true witness, the ruler of God's cre-
    ation (3:14)
the Lion of the tribe of Judah (5:5)
the Root of David (5:5)
the spirit of prophecy (19:10)
a rider on a white horse who is called Faithful and True . . . whose
    eyes are like blazing fire, and on whose head are many crowns
    (19:11-12)
one dressed in a white robe dipped in blood, whose name is the
    Word of God (19:13)
one who rules with an iron scepter (19:15)
King of kings and Lord of lords (19:16)
the Root and Offspring of David (22:16)
the bright Morning Star (22:16)

In only the opening chapters, mostly in the letters to the seven churches of Asia Minor, a similarly spectacular panoply of actions is ascribed to Jesus:

he loves us and has freed us from our sins by his blood (1:5)
he has made us to be a kingdom of priests to serve his God and
    Father (1:6)
he holds the seven stars in his right hand and walks among the
    seven golden lampstands (2:1)
he wields a sharp, double-edged sword (2:12)
he will rule the nations with an iron scepter; he will dash them in
    pieces like pottery (2:27)
he holds the seven spirits of God and the seven stars (3:1)
he will come like a thief, and none will know at what time he will
    arrive (3:3)

he holds the key of David (3:7)

he is about to spit the lukewarm out of his mouth (3:16)

he stands at the door and knocks (3:20)

Yet this is not all. Indefatigably, Revelation piles on image after image, or — even more provocatively — turns a single image into a kaleidoscope of tropes. So it is especially with the depiction of Jesus as a Lamb. Assuming that the author of Revelation is the same John who penned the Gospel, or at least that they share a common Johannine community, we have an expanded riff in the former on words from the first chapter of the latter that describe Jesus as "the Lamb of God, who takes away the sin of the world" (John 1:29) — which was itself already an interpretation of the Old Testament system of sacrifice as now recapitulated in the existence of a single person. In Revelation the depiction of the Lamb runs wild:

A Lamb, "looking as if it had been slain," is now pictured as a seven-eyed and seven-horned creature who sends the seven spirits of God into all the earth, who opens a powerful scroll, and who receives tumultuous adulation (5:6-10).

The Lamb opens seals that no one else can touch (6:1).

The Lamb's holy anger burns so hot against "the kings of the earth, the princes, the generals, the rich, the mighty, and every slave and every free man" that they beseech the mountains to cover them so as to escape "the wrath of the Lamb" (6:15-16).

In the very next chapter the same Lamb appears as a tender shepherd who leads his people to living water and wipes every tear from their eyes (7:17).

The blood of the Lamb inspires his followers, even as they face death, to overcome "the accuser" (12:10-11).

Those who triumphed over the beast join to sing "the song of Moses the servant of God and the song of the Lamb" (15:3).

Ultimately, the Lamb overcomes all God's enemies because "he is Lord of lords and King of kings" (17:14).

In the climactic celebration of the transition from the world as it has been to the new heaven and new earth, the servants of God proclaim joyfully that "the wedding of the Lamb has come, / and his bride [the church] has made herself ready" (19:7).

And at the end of all things it is said that the New Jerusalem contains no temple because "the Lord God Almighty and the Lamb are its temple," and there is no need for sun or moon, "for the glory of God gives it light, and the Lamb is its lamp" (21:22-23).

Remembering that the book of Revelation is only one relatively small part of the New Testament witness to Jesus Christ and that its picture of Jesus Christ as the Lamb of God is only one image in that book, we are still confronted with a dazzling catalogue of images for Jesus: sacrifice — seven-horned victor — magus — wrathful scourge — tender shepherd — Lord of lords and King of kings — bridegroom — temple — light.

The figure of Christ, displayed with such extraordinary multiplicity, was at the center of the new religion that spread out of Judea — and out of a culture shaped by the religion of Israel. It spread into a Roman world of orderly laws and brutal armies overlaid by a Hellenistic intellectual culture of speculative philosophy and painstaking ethical precision. In such circumstances it became imperative for internal self-understanding, external proclamation, and defensive apologetics to synthesize the profuse biblical material making up this new religion that had emerged from ancient Judaism. The creeds responded to that necessity.

Creeds as Foundations

In the early Christian centuries believers dealt in many ways with the realities they believed God had displayed in Scripture and in the person of Christ. Those realities provided the material for worship, they became the driving force leading to conversions, they were the source of great comfort in the face of deadly peril, and they were at the root of endless conflicts among believers themselves. The business of those who composed the creeds was to organize the experiences of faith — of word, deed, worship, prayer, hymn, witness, consolation, debate — into formulas that could speak for the church to the world while also describing the church's most basic affirmations to its own adherents. Creeds were by no means all that contributed to the health of early Christian communities, but they played a major part. Because of their importance — summarizing the Scriptures authoritatively and clarifying key points of confusion — the major creeds became securely established as reliable guides for what it meant to be Christian. That authority, in turn, is what has made them through the centuries so useful for so many purposes, including (in our own day) the purposes of Christian learning.

Many reliable accounts exist to explain the complicated twists and turns that led to the major statements of Christian faith.[2] For our purposes, the history behind the creeds is not as pertinent as their main affirmations. But a word or two of history is useful for understanding the questions these authoritative statements were trying to answer.

The Apostles' Creed

The Apostles' Creed did not achieve its final form until the seventh century, but its main assertions had been clearly anticipated by earlier creedal-type statements. Thus, as early as about A.D. 110, Ignatius, an early bishop of Antioch in Syria, summarized the Christian faith in one of his letters. His précis anticipated much of what

2. See especially *Creeds and Confessions of Faith in the Christian Tradition,* ed. Jaroslav Pelikan and Valerie Hotchkiss (New Haven: Yale University Press, 2003), with three volumes of carefully edited texts and commentary on individual creeds and a fourth volume as Pelikan's monograph on the creeds, their importance, and their use. A superlative general history is J. N. D. Kelly, *Early Christian Doctrines,* 5th ed. (New York: Continuum, 2000). My own interpretation of the creeds set in the broader perspective of early Christian history is found in *Turning Points: Decisive Moments in the History of Christianity,* 2nd ed. (Grand Rapids: Baker, 2000), 23-82.

would later be found in this statement of faith: "Turn a deaf ear to any speaker who avoids mention of Jesus Christ who was of David's line, born of Mary, who was truly born, ate and drank; was truly persecuted under Pontius Pilate, truly crucified and died while those in heaven, on earth, and under the earth beheld it; who also was truly raised from the dead, the Father having raised him, who in like manner will raise us also who believe in him — his Father, I say, will raise us in Christ Jesus, apart from whom we have not true life."[3]

The Apostles' Creed and early statements anticipating it responded not so much to doctrinal disputes as to the need for baptismal teaching. Those who were to be baptized, which usually took place at Easter, answered questions about God the Father, God the Son, and God the Holy Spirit. The digest of Christian teaching with which baptismal candidates responded gradually evolved into this creed:

> I believe in God, the Father Almighty, Creator of heaven and earth.
>
> And in Jesus Christ, his only Son, our Lord, who was conceived of the Holy Spirit, born of the Virgin Mary, suffered under Pontius Pilate, was crucified, died, and was buried; he descended into hell. On the third day he rose from the dead; he ascended into heaven, sits at the right hand of God the Father Almighty. Thence he shall come to judge the living and the dead.
>
> I believe in the Holy Spirit, the holy catholic church, the communion of saints, the forgiveness of sins, the resurrection of the body, and the life everlasting. Amen.[4]

Although polemical combat was not the main intent, the creed did make several crucial doctrinal affirmations. The world created by God; the work accomplished by Jesus; the institutions, deeds, and expectations inspired by the Holy Spirit — all were manifestations of the one true God. Moreover, Jesus was the "Christ," or Messiah, who fulfilled Old Testament expectations; he was the One who lived, died, and rose again from the dead for all humans.

---

3. Ignatius, *Letter to the Trallians,* in *The Early Christian Fathers,* ed. Henry Bettenson (London: Oxford University Press, 1956), 60-61.

4. *Creeds and Confessions,* 1:669.

As a guide to Christian intellectual life, the Apostles' Creed constructs a particularly important foundation. It brings together in an entirely fruitful way confidence in God the creator of the material realm and God the Father of believers through the saving work of Christ. In turn, that combination offers precisely the tension Christian scholarship requires between life focused on this world and life convinced of the world to come. The creed, thus, offers full cause for taking seriously the fact of the physical world as created by God, but also the drama of redemption that relativizes all terrestrial realities in eternal perspective. It offers, in short, an ideal place from which to approach the tasks of Christian learning.

The Nicene Creed

The complicated background of the so-called Nicene Creed deserves extensive exposition, but for our purposes can be sketched briefly.[5] By the early fourth century the Christian faith had spread widely around the Mediterranean basin, and well beyond. Circulation of the Scriptures — now a New Testament about Christ completing the Old Testament revelation to Israel — created strong connections among Christian communities. Development of a system of church governance by bishops had much the same effect because the bishops were able to organize local communities of believers while also providing a measure of communication from one Christian location to another. The hostility of the Roman Empire remained a pressing difficulty, but even more pressing were divergent interpretations of Christ and his work. Where the former threatened the church with persecution, the latter threatened it with intellectual and religious chaos.

Already deeply ingrained in the believing community, however, were practices that reflected the New Testament witness to Christ as sharing fully the glory of God. Entrance into the community through baptism took place in the name of the Trinity — Father, Son, and Holy Spirit. Many of the church's first hymns praised Jesus as the one who,

---

5. For a fuller account, see my *Turning Points,* 47-64.

acting for God and as God, brought salvation to humanity. But against these practices — which had been given theological shape by leaders such as Tertullian of Carthage (ca. 167–ca. 225), who coined the term "Trinity" — there existed what might be called the powerful logic of monotheism. Especially as the faith spread through Hellenistic regions, where painstaking intellectual reflection was a given way of life, more and more formulas were advanced to explain the relationship between the man Jesus and the one true God.

Some of these formulas were as ingenious as they were troubling to the instincts of worshiping communities. They included proposals that treated all revelations of God as three successive manifestations of the same divine Being — first Father, then Son, finally Spirit. Others sought to preserve monotheism by describing Jesus as far better, far more holy, and far more conscious of God than any other human, but as still a creature distinct in his essence from the one God. Among those who argued for this latter view most persuasively was a scholar-priest from Alexandria in North Africa whose teachings attracted unusual attention in the first decades of the fourth century.

This priest was Arius (ca. 250–ca. 336), who brought thorough knowledge of the Scriptures and great respect for Jesus to his work. To Arius, New Testament statements about Jesus going hungry, or growing in knowledge, showed that he could not be fully divine, since to be perfect and unchanging in all attributes was simply what it meant to be God. While Arius thought it was appropriate to call Jesus "the first-born of creation" — which in fact the apostle Paul had done — it was not appropriate to see Jesus as the absolutely changeless, perfect, transcendent One.

Arius's teaching won some followers and caused much consternation. Significantly, it began to spread just when the church's relation to the Roman Empire underwent an unprecedented reversal. The emergence of Emperor Constantine from a tangled competition for power changed forever the history of Christianity. (Constantine became the sole emperor in 312.) Through a series of dramatic events, including Constantine's vision of a cross in heaven, the emperor became a patron of the faith. Although official patronage would come to entangle the church in many difficulties, at the time it seemed noth-

15

ing short of miraculous that the hostility of the world's greatest political power toward the church could be turned into support for the church.

Whatever the difficulties that resulted when Rome became a friend to Christ, one immediate payoff was that Constantine's favor allowed the church's bishops to meet together to adjudicate their common problems. Not since Jesus' handpicked disciples met in Jerusalem after his death had it been possible for the leaders of the church to gather in this way. The first matter they addressed in taking advantage of this opportunity was the challenge of Arius's teaching about Jesus.

So it was that in the year 325 in Nicea, a bustling city near Constantine's military headquarters in Asia Minor (site of the town of Iznik in modern Turkey), about 230 bishops gathered to address the question of how best to formulate the relationship of Jesus Christ to God the Father (and also to address a number of controversial practical issues, like fixing the date for Easter). After serious deliberation and the direct urging of Constantine — who wanted the faith clarified and a clarified faith to support his own efforts as emperor — the bishops agreed upon a short formula.

The main points of this formula rebuked Arius's speculations in order to state in clear-cut phrases what had been widely intuited in the worshiping practices of the church. Jesus Christ was *true God from true God.* He was *begotten, not made.* He was *consubstantial* (= of one substance) *with the Father* (some held back from affirming this proposition, not because they did not believe it, but because the Greek word for "consubstantial," *homoousios,* was not itself a New Testament word). And *for us humans and for our salvation he came down and became incarnate, became human.*[6]

The struggle, however, was far from over. Advocates of Arian opinions continued to press their views and to oppose the conclusions of the council. After Constantine's death in 337, other emperors found reasons for supporting Arian positions and advocates. The fact that words like *homoousios* were not in the Bible continued to trouble

---

6. Quotations from *Creeds and Confessions,* 1:159.

some. And since the statement of Nicea made only passing reference to the Holy Spirit, it opened the door to new and troubling opinions about the person of the Spirit and the work of the Spirit.

Considerable controversy accompanied by vicious ecclesiastical infighting was the result. But through the tumult, the enduring note was a combination of convictions — concerning the person of Christ as Savior and concerning the saving work of Christ embodied in his person. Athanasius (ca. 296-373), who became bishop of Alexandria after the council adjourned, was the great champion of this position. In countless speeches, letters, and tracts, and in the face of great opposition, Athanasius held to the Nicene standard: "He, the Mighty One, the Artificer [Creator] of all, Himself prepared this body in the virgin as a temple for Himself, and took it for His very own, as the instrument through which He was known and in which He dwelt. Thus, taking a body like our own, because all our bodies were liable to the corruption of death, He surrendered His body to death in place of all, and offered it to the Father. This He did out of sheer love for us, so that in His death all might die, and the law of death thereby be abolished."[7]

Finally, in 381 at another council (this one at Constantinople) called by another emperor (Theodosius), bishops met once again and issued an expansion of the Nicene formula that was intended both to respect the key teachings of the earlier statement and to flesh out answers to later objections. This document is what is now known as the Nicene Creed:

> We believe in one God the Father all-powerful, Maker of heaven and of earth, and of all things both seen and unseen. And in one Lord Jesus Christ, the only-begotten Son of God, begotten from the Father before all the ages, light from light, true God from true God, begotten not made, consubstantial with the Father, through whom all things came to be; for us humans and for our salvation he came down from the heavens and became incarnate from the Holy Spirit and the Virgin Mary, became human and was crucified on our behalf under Pontius Pilate; he suffered and was buried and rose up

7. *St. Athanasius on the Incarnation,* introduction by C. S. Lewis (Crestwood, NY: St. Vladimir's Orthodox Theological Seminary, 1953; original 1944), 34.

on the third day in accordance with the Scriptures; and he went up into the heavens and is seated at the Father's right hand; he is coming again with glory to judge the living and the dead; his kingdom will have no end. And in the Spirit, the holy, the lordly, and life-giving one, proceeding forth from the Father, co-worshiped and co-glorified with Father and Son, the one who spoke through the prophets; in one, holy, catholic, and apostolic church. We confess one baptism for the forgiving of sins. We look forward to a resurrection of the dead and life in the age to come. Amen.[8]

The Nicene Creed has been a bedrock foundation for Christian worship and theological reflection for over 1,600 years, and in all the major Christian traditions. It provides for the tasks of human learning the same solid foundation it does for all other tasks. For the sake of intellectual activity, it was especially momentous that the creed linked its affirmation of the full divinity of Christ — "light from light, true God from true God, . . . consubstantial with the Father" — with the confession that Christ was incarnate "for us humans and for our salvation." In other words, the gift of salvation, upon which the destiny of humanity hung, was accomplished by the incarnation (life, death, and resurrection) of the Son of God.

The specific contribution of Nicea to Christian learning is to affirm that God accomplished human salvation through the incarnation, and that the incarnation's full revelation of God took place in the materiality and through the events of this world. Jesus was not just God-like but "true God from true God." Moreover, he did not just *seem* to have a life on earth, but, for the sake of his people and their salvation, he truly entered into ordinary human history. The narrative summarized by the creed, which shows God making the fullest revelation of himself *in* the created world and *through* events occurring in that world, is of highest significance for revealing the path of salvation. But by extension, that narrative also implies something very positive about the created world and the human events, structures, and institutions found in that world. If the world and human culture consti-

---

8. *Creeds and Confessions*, 1:163.

tute the venue that God chose to reveal himself in Christ and accomplish his great work of salvation through Christ, then that world and culture have been lent an extraordinary dignity — not in and of themselves, but as the God-blessed arenas of redemption.

The Definition of Chalcedon

Deliberations at Nicea and Constantinople settled a great deal concerning the person and work of Christ, but the very clarity of the creed concerning the divinity of Christ also raised further questions of supreme importance: If Jesus was fully divine, how was he also human? If Jesus was somehow both human and divine, how was it possible to speak about Jesus' person without making him out to be a freak of human nature, a compromise of deity, or both?[9]

Another tangled period of controversy, proposal, counterproposal, imperial meddling, imperial assistance, and interecclesiastical strife followed. One strong opinion with many supporters held that Jesus should indeed be viewed as a single entity (Word-Flesh Christology), but this solution seemed to imply something deficient about Jesus' humanity and something lacking about his divinity. Another strong opinion held that it was of first importance to affirm that Jesus possessed a fully divine nature and a fully human nature (Word-Man Christology), but this solution seemed to imply that Jesus was a split personality divided into two discrete halves.

Difficulties in resolving such problems required sorting through Latin and Greek shades of difference on key terms like "nature," "flesh," "substance," and "person." They also included the difficult recognition that some aspects of the divine reality in and of Christ could only be described and never fully comprehended. Once again the way out of the dilemma was marked by those who saw most clearly that the theology of the church must be guided by its worship of Jesus Christ as Savior and Master. So it was with the famous *Tome* of Pope Leo I, which he promulgated in 449 as a way of explaining why a theol-

---

9. For a fuller account, see my *Turning Points*, 65-82.

ogy of Christ's person must reflect the saving reality of his work. Leo stressed the fact that the hope of the whole world hinged on Christ possessing two natures (even two substances) in one integrated person: "as our salvation requires, one and the same mediator between God and human beings, the human being who is Jesus Christ, can at one and the same time die in virtue of the one nature and, in virtue of the other, be incapable of death. That is why true God was born in the integral and complete nature of a true human being, entire in what belongs to him and entire in what belongs to us."[10]

Guided by mediating voices like Leo's, the more than 500 bishops who met in 451 at Chalcedon (modern Kadıköy), across the Bosporus from Constantinople, hammered out the following definition:

> So, following the saintly fathers, we all with one voice teach the confession of one and the same Son, our Lord Jesus Christ: the same perfect in divinity and perfect in humanity, the same truly God and truly man, of a rational soul and a body; consubstantial with the Father as regards his divinity, and the same consubstantial with us as regards his humanity; like us in all respects except for sin; begotten before the ages from the Father as regards his divinity, and in the last days the same for us and for our salvation from Mary, the Virgin God-bearer as regards his humanity; one and the same Christ, Son, Lord, Only-begotten, acknowledged in two natures which undergo no confusion, no change, no division, no separation; at no point was the difference between the natures taken away through the union, but rather the property of both natures is preserved and comes together into a single person and a single subsistent being; he is not parted or divided into two persons, but is one and the same only-begotten Son, God, Word, Lord Jesus Christ, just as the prophets taught from the beginning about him, and as the Lord Jesus Christ himself instructed us, and as the creed of the fathers [i.e., the Nicene Creed] handed it down to us.[11]

10. Pope Leo I's Letter, in *The Christological Controversy*, ed. Richard A. Norris (Philadelphia: Fortress, 1980), 148.
11. *Creeds and Confessions*, 1:181.

The Definition of Chalcedon was different from the Nicene Creed because it did not so much define doctrine as fence it in. To reflect what Christ had accomplished for the salvation of sinners, it was necessary to affirm that the unity of his one person encompassed full humanity and full divinity. But how exactly the fullness of humanity and divinity could exist in an integrated person was left unexplained. The important thing was the church's affirmation that it was sticking to its experience of what had happened, even if it could not fully explain the details of how exactly what had happened had indeed occurred.

The great gift of Chalcedon to Christian scholarship is to show how basic for the truth of all things is the consubstantiality between the divine and the human, a consubstantiality that is resolved (but not fully explained) in Jesus Christ. The Definition steered a course between extremes. To stress too much the divine reality present within human life would have moved toward a superspiritual gnostic literalism (gnosticism, an ancient heresy, claimed that only certain adepts could see the true nature of all things as essentially spiritual and also recognize the gross unreality of the human or material realm). To stress too much the human shape of divine revelation within the world would have moved toward a water-thin modernism (a recent heresy maintaining that only certain learned rationalists could see the true character of all things as essentially natural and also recognize the mythic unreality of the supernatural realm). By contrast to these heresies, if the tension of Chalcedon could be maintained — fully divine and fully human in one integrated entity — believers possessed the most solid basis imaginable for the union of true Christianity (grounded in divine realities) and true scholarship (grounded in interaction with the world), and, in the words of Chalcedon, with "no confusion, no change, no division, no separation."

Putting Theology to Work

What can be drawn from the creeds? The Christian traditions that have embraced these ancient formulas, as well as the classic theologies that the creeds have anchored, provide the scope and the depth required for practicing a Christian scholarship worthy of the name. They offer believers the stuff needed for engaging minds for Christ. Thus, the greatest hope for Christian learning in our age, or in any age, lies not primarily in heightened activity, in better funding, or in strategizing for the tasks at hand — though all these matters play an important part. Rather, the great hope for Christian learning is to delve deeper into the Christian faith itself. And going deeper into the Christian faith means, in the end, learning more of Jesus Christ.

Evangelical Christians, in particular, do not necessarily need to abandon the activism, the emphasis on conversion, or the democratic biblicism that define evangelical history in order to pursue the life of the mind. But if evangelicals are to make a genuinely Christian contribution to intellectual life, they must ground faith in the great traditions of classical Christian theology, for these are the traditions that reveal the heights and depths of Jesus Christ. Intellectually, there is no other way.

But how to go about that task? How is it possible to pursue goals defined by lofty phrases like "first-rate Christian scholarship" or "the Christian use of the mind" when those words sound to some in the church like backsliding and to many outside the church like simple oxymorons? For Christian believers, the only possible answer must come from considering Jesus Christ.

This claim rests on convictions about who Jesus Christ was and is. Since the reality of Jesus Christ sustains the world and all that is in it, so too should the reality of Jesus Christ sustain the most wholehearted, unabashed, and unembarrassed efforts to understand the world and all that is in it. The Light of the World, the Word of God, the Son of Man, the True Vine, the Bread of Life, the Bright and Morning Star — for believers, this One is the Savior, but also the Paradigm. Whatever is true of the world in general must also be true for those parts of the world that emphasize intellectual life. The light of Christ illuminates the laboratory, his speech is the fount of communication, he makes possible the study of humans in all their interactions, he is the source of all life, he provides the wherewithal for every achievement of human civilization, he is the telos of all that is beautiful. He is, among his many other titles, the Christ of the Academic Road.

TWO

Jesus Christ: Motives for Serious Learning

—⟋⟋⟋—

E vangelical Christians are often faulted for treating the Bible as a mechanical bequest from the skies in which verses function like puzzle pieces to be assembled according to the reader's predetermined assumptions about what God is like and how he must act. This charge is not groundless, although it can be pointed out that such evangelical excesses only reverse the reflexes of some secular readers whose presuppositions rule out — without serious investigation or even much thought — any supernatural presence in the content of the Bible or its composition.

In this chapter I risk approaching the caricature of forced evangelical interpretation by using selected New Testament passages concerning the person and work of Jesus Christ to draw out intellectual implications from the christological affirmations of the creeds. If patient exegesis was the main purpose of this book, and if I had the expertise to carry out such work, I am confident that disciplined scholarship would more or less confirm the conclusions drawn below. But since the main point of this book is to encourage those who already accept traditional interpretations of the Bible, and since I do not possess the requisite skills for technical exegesis, brief exploration of the texts must suffice.

The important points do not, however, require elaborate exegetical enterprise. If only a fraction of the rapid survey that follows is true — if the conclusions below reflect only a partial grasp of the Scriptures — it would be enough to establish the overwhelming importance of Jesus Christ for the tasks of human learning. In 1960 Jaroslav Pelikan described "the virtues of the Christian intellectual" in Trinitarian terms that parallel the arguments advanced here. In his rendering, those virtues included "a passion for being because the Father is the Creator and Source of all being; a reverence for language because Jesus Christ is the Word and Mind of the Father; an enthusiasm for history because the Holy Spirit works through history to produce variety and to unite all men to himself."[1] In a simpler, more directly christological approach, I am pointing to the same conclusions.

"Through Whom He Made the Universe": The Origin of All Things in Christ

The New Testament could not be clearer in its multiple affirmations about the role of Christ in creating the world. Significantly, the same message comes in different ways from different voices in the New Testament canon. That message is straightforward and direct: a Christian doctrine of creation must be christological. So from the first chapter of John: "He [the Word] was with God in the beginning. Through him all things were made; without him nothing was made that has been made" (John 1:2-3). So also it appears from the apostle Paul, as in the first chapter of the Epistle to the Colossians: Christ is "the image of the invisible God, the firstborn over all creation. For by him all things were created: things in heaven and on earth, visible and invisible, whether thrones or powers or rulers or authorities: all things were created by him and for him" (Col. 1:15-16). The same message comes from the author of the Epistle to the Hebrews: "In these last days," God has spoken conclusively "by his Son, whom he appointed heir of all things, and through whom he made the universe" (Heb. 1:2).

1. Jaroslav Pelikan, "A Portrait of a Christian as a Young Intellectual," *The Cresset,* Trinity 2005, p. 65 (from a commencement address delivered at Valparaiso University, June 6, 1960).

Oceans of commentary have been written on these passages, much concerning the possibility that New Testament writers were borrowing Platonic or Neoplatonic notions of a Demiurge through whom the eternal and unchanging Spirit of Pure Form bequeathed order to the chaos of the material world. Whether such borrowings took place or not is a consequential matter. Even more important is what such passages affirm.

That affirmation carries the strongest possible implications for intellectual life. Put most simply, for believers to be studying created things is to be studying the works of Christ. For the argument that the second person of the Trinity was the active agent in the divine creation of the world, it does not follow that his work of redemption was less important. Loyalty to the reality of Christ the Redeemer does not require disloyalty to the reality of Christ as Creator.

Taking this strand of New Testament teaching seriously reveals the world in a new light. There simply is nothing humanly possible to study about the created realm that, *in principle,* leads us away from Jesus Christ. To be sure, humans may misunderstand knowledge gained by studying the world, put it to evil uses, transform it into an idol, or otherwise abuse it. But these shortcomings do not alter the fact that, in the biblical view, the world was brought into existence by Jesus Christ.

The Catholic theologian Robert Barron recently summarized well the implications for learning that flow from a "high Christology," that is, a Christology that insists on both the complete deity and the complete humanity of Jesus. "Because Jesus Christ is the Logos incarnate — and not simply another interesting religious figure among many — signs of his presence and style are found everywhere, and he can relate noncompetitively to them." Barron goes on to suggest that "the higher the Christology," the more payoff for learning, since "it is precisely the epistemic priority of Jesus Christ, the Word made flesh, that warrants the use of philosophical and cultural tools in the explication and propagation of the faith, since those means come from and lead to the very Word."[2]

---

2. Robert Barron, *The Priority of Christ: Toward a Postliberal Catholicism* (Grand Rapids: Baker, 2007), 152.

The Irish poet Evangeline Patterson expressed the same liberation found in acknowledging Christ as the Creating Word when she wrote about her own experience: "I was brought up in a Christian movement where, because God had to be given pre-eminence, nothing else was allowed to be important. I have broken through to the position that because God exists, everything else has significance."[3] In sum, to confess Christ is to make an extraordinarily strong statement about the value of studying the things Christ has made.

"In Him All Things Consist": The Comprehensiveness of Jesus as the Word of God

For Christian believers who pursue an academic vocation, Paul's letter to the Colossians should be a central text, especially for how it expands upon the Christ-centered creation of the world. In particular, we have from verse 13 in chapter 1 a memorable conjunction of affirmations with much to ponder for anyone engaged in any facet of intellectual life. The complex interconnections of the passage require full quotation:

> He [God] has rescued us from the dominion of darkness and brought us into the kingdom of the Son he loves, in whom we have redemption, the forgiveness of sins.
>
> He is the image of the invisible God, the firstborn over all creation. For by him all things were created: things in heaven and on earth, visible and invisible, whether thrones or powers or rulers or authorities; all things were created by him and for him. He is before all things, and in him all things hold together. And he is the head of the body, the church; he is the beginning and the firstborn from among the dead, so that in everything he might have the supremacy. For God was pleased to have all his fullness dwell in him, and through him to reconcile to himself all things, whether things

3. Joy Alexander, "In Conversation with Evangeline Patterson," *Journal of the Irish Christian Study Centre* 4 (1989): 42.

on earth or things in heaven, by making peace through his blood, shed on the cross. . . .

I want you to know how much I am struggling for you and for those at Laodicea, and for all who have not met me personally. My purpose is that they may be encouraged in heart and united in love, so that they may have the full riches of complete understanding, in order that they may know the mystery of God, namely, Christ, in whom are hidden all the treasures of wisdom and knowledge. (Col. 1:13-20; 2:1-3)

The guiding message of this passage would seem to be clear: the lordship of Christ over all things is inextricably related to the salvation offered through his work on the cross. There is no point in talking about Christian scholarship without first talking about the need to be Christian. The final hope of believing intellectuals or academics is no different from the hope of believers of any sort. And that hope is found in the one who makes "peace through the blood of the cross."

The passage in Colossians explicitly exalts the person and work of Christ as the key to human salvation; implicitly it affirms that salvation is the overwhelmingly central concern of human existence. To be rescued from darkness and transferred to the kingdom of God's Son is what it means for the Son to provide redemption, the forgiveness of sin. Such a rescue by such a savior deserves to be the most important concern of all humans everywhere and in all times.

But precisely within the framework provided by this proclamation of salvation, and interwoven seamlessly with soteriological realities, come other statements, which are almost as remarkable, about the meaning of Jesus Christ for everything else. Thus, Christ is not only the firstborn in creation, but he is also the source and energy of all things, for everything was created in him and for him. The extent of Christ's creative work, according to the apostle, is universal. Whether we consider realms of the spirit or realms of nature (things "in heaven and on earth"), external life or internal life (things "visible and invisible"), the interactions of humans with spiritual realities or with other humans ("whether thrones or powers or rulers or authorities") — in other words, the stuff of academic study in all its diversity — we are

27

dealing with the effulgence of Jesus Christ. In the passage, the apostle Paul moves rapidly, effortlessly, and without even pausing for breath between describing the salvation that Christian believers find in their Redeemer and depicting the cosmic scope of what is "held together" through that same Redeemer.

The claims are striking and bear repeating. The apostle says, in effect, that if we study anything in the realms of nature or the realms of the spirit, we study what came into existence through Jesus Christ. Likewise, if we study human interactions or spiritual-human interactions (thrones, dominions, rulers, powers), we are studying realms brought into existence by Jesus Christ. If our study concerns predictability, uniformity, regularity, we are working in the domains of the one who "is before all things, and [in whom] all things hold together." If our study concerns beauty, power, or agency, it is the same, "for God was pleased to have all his fullness dwell in him." And if we succeed to any degree, we are only following after Jesus Christ, "in whom are hidden all the treasures of wisdom and knowledge."

This passage in Colossians lies behind a question that the Presbyterian theologian B. B. Warfield once posed to a group of seminarians who assumed that pursuits of study and pursuits of godliness could not function together: "Why should you turn from God when you turn to your books, or feel that you must turn from your books in order to turn to God?"[4]

Of the many other faithful commentators who have stretched language in order to capture the stunning reach of the apostle's message, I am selecting only two more. So from John Piper:

> All that came into being exists for Christ — that is, everything exists to display the greatness of Christ. Nothing — nothing! — in the universe exists for its own sake. Everything — from the bottom of the oceans to the top of the mountains, from the smallest particle to the biggest star, from the most boring school subject to the

---

4. B. B. Warfield, "The Religious Life of Theological Students" (an address at Princeton Theological Seminary, 1911), quoted here from *Selected Shorter Writings of B. B. Warfield*, ed. John E. Meeter, 2 vols. (Phillipsburg, NJ: Presbyterian and Reformed, 1970), 412.

most fascinating science, from the ugliest cockroach to the most beautiful human, from the greatest saint to the most wicked genocidal dictator — everything that exists, exists to make the greatness of Christ more fully known — including *you,* and the person you have the hardest time liking.[5]

Again, from N. T. Wright:

There is no sphere of existence over which Jesus is not sovereign, in virtue of his role both in creation (1:16-17) and in reconciliation (1:18-20). There can be no dualistic division between some areas which he rules and others which he does not. "There is no neutral ground in the universe: every square inch, every split second, is claimed by God and counterclaimed by Satan." The task of evangelism is therefore best understood as the proclamation that Jesus is already Lord, that in him God's new creation has broken into history, and that all people are therefore summoned to submit to him in love, worship, and obedience. The logic of this message requires that those who announce it should be seeking to bring Christ's Lordship to bear on every area of human and worldly existence.[6]

Such claims about the origin and sustaining of all things in Christ are coordinated in the Colossians passage with the message of salvation. Because those who trust in Christ for salvation are defined so completely by that message, they should be the first to explore what Christ has made and what his ongoing power sustains. If this passage was believed, it would never be appropriate to set matters of salvation and matters of wisdom or knowledge in opposition. Priorities or urgent necessities would still matter in how redemption and wisdom are arranged against each other, but as a matter of principle these two di-

5. John Piper, *Spectacular Sins: And Their Global Purpose in the Glory of Christ* (Wheaton, IL: Crossway, 2007), 33.

6. N. T. Wright, *The Epistles of Paul to the Colossians and to Philemon: An Introduction and Commentary,* Tyndale New Testament Commentaries (Grand Rapids: Eerdmans, 1986), 79-80. The quotation is from C. S. Lewis, "Christianity and Culture," in Lewis's *Christian Reflections,* ed. Walter Hooper (Grand Rapids: Eerdmans, 1967), 33.

mensions of reality could not conflict. Rather, both the salvation won by Christ and the study of "all things" would be viewed as intimately related to each other because both are dependent upon Jesus Christ.

But there is still more to say. Because for a Christian the tasks of scholarship are tied so closely to the unearned gift of salvation, there can be no genuine Christian learning that is arrogant, self-justifying, imperious, or callous to the human needs of colleagues, students, and the broader public. The tight conjunction of assertions in Colossians underscores the fact that all humans, including academics, are needy sinners who require God. All humans, including academics, remain in need of divine grace even as they explore the depths of "wisdom and knowledge" hidden in Jesus Christ.

Not coincidentally, Paul in this same passage also says important things about the community of faith: that Christ "is the head of the body, the church" (Col. 1:18). And that in Paul's own "flesh" he fills up "what is still lacking in regard to Christ's affliction, for the sake of his body, which is the church" (Col. 1:24). The apostle joins consideration of the church to a description of the salvation won by Christ on the cross and to an understanding of the rule of Jesus Christ over all things. By so doing he points believers to the corporate nature of life and to the historical character of human existence. By implication, if Christ-sanctified human learning is parallel to Christ-accomplished human salvation, then corporate and historical relationships are as foundational to the enterprise of learning as they are to the existence of the church.

In sum, to follow the apostle Paul as he reasons about Christ in the first and second chapters of Colossians is to encounter a bracing and multidimensional reality. The name of the reality is Jesus Christ. The scope of the reality is boundless.

"He Will Never Leave You": The Christian Doctrine of Providence

The Christian doctrine of providence restates what it means for all things to "hold together" in Christ. With this theme, however, the perspective moves away from the activity of the Son to the energetic oversight of the Father. This doctrine, where Christology plays an indirect but no less powerful role, should also communicate great confidence in pursuing intellectual tasks. From the perspective of providence, everything that exists is sustained by the wisdom and power of God. The way that acknowledging God as the origin of all things leads on to recognizing providence (or God's active rule over all things) was put very well in the Belgic Confession of 1561. In its statements, this confession also shows how general revelation (what humans know by studying the world) can be connected to special revelation (what they know by studying the Bible). In explaining the "means" by which "we know God," the confession affirmed that "We know him by two means: First, by the creation, preservation, and government of the universe, since that universe is before our eyes like a beautiful book, in which all creatures, great and small, are like letters to make us ponder the invisible things of God: his eternal power and his divinity, as the apostle Paul says in Romans 1.20. . . . Second, he makes himself known to us more openly by his holy and divine word, as much as we need in this life, for his glory and for the salvation of his own."[7]

By speaking of God's preservation and government of the universe, the Belgic Confession attempted to capture the dynamism of God's present rule over the earth. The intellectual implications of that rule are also hinted at many times in the Scriptures, as for example in Psalm 19, when the psalmist personified inanimate forces of nature:

> The heavens declare the glory of God;
>> the skies proclaim the work of his hands.
> Day after day they pour forth speech;
>> night after night they display knowledge.
> There is no speech or language
>> where their voice is not heard.
> Their voice goes out into all the earth,
>> their words to the ends of the world.
>
> (Ps. 19:1-4)

7. *Creeds and Confessions of Faith in the Christian Tradition,* ed. Jaroslav Pelikan and Valerie Hotchkiss, 3 vols. (New Haven: Yale University Press, 2003), 2:407.

The same sense of dynamic, all-encompassing providence infuses passages from the New Testament, like 1 Timothy 4:4-5: "Everything God created is good, and nothing is to be rejected if it is received with thanksgiving, because it is consecrated by the word of God and prayer." These scriptural descriptions of God's active, loving, energetic, and beautiful providence have provided rich themes for many pious minds, but few as telling as the energy that the English Catholic poet Gerard Manley Hopkins once pictured like this:

> The world is charged with the grandeur of God;
> It will flame out like shining from shook foil.[8]

But what is the christological meaning of a doctrine of providence that features the Creator God's care over what he has made? The surest proof offered in Scripture for the contention that God rules *everything* is the divine testament, ratified by the death of his Son, that "he will never leave *you* nor forsake *you.*" In the Bible this promise appears in two very different contexts. We hear the words first as an encouragement to ancient Israel not to fear the military might of its foes: "Be strong and courageous. Do not be afraid or terrified because of them, for the LORD your God goes with you; he will never leave you nor forsake you" (Deut. 31:6). Then at the end of the book of Hebrews, which was written to show how God's work in Christ had absorbed and excelled his work from ancient days, the same words reappear as a general exhortation not to worry about amassing great worldly treasure: "Keep your lives free from the love of money and be content with what you have, for God has said, 'Never will I leave you; / never will I forsake you.' So we say with confidence, 'The Lord is my helper; I will not be afraid. / What can man do to me?'" (Heb. 13:5-6). The final quotation, which the author of Hebrews uses to complete the circle by referencing another promise made to ancient Israel, comes from Psalm 118:

> The LORD is with me; I will not be afraid.
> What can man do to me?

8. Gerard Manley Hopkins, "God's Grandeur," in *A Critical Edition of the Major Works,* ed. Catherine Phillips (New York: Oxford University Press, 1986), 128.

The LORD is with me; he is my helper.
I will look in triumph on my enemies.

(Ps. 118:6-7)

The message conveyed by such passages has been the theme of countless Christian statements, but none so effective as the Heidelberg Catechism of the sixteenth century. Its opening words affirm that the Christian's only comfort in life and in death is "that I belong . . . not to myself but to my faithful Savior, Jesus Christ . . . ; indeed, that everything must fit his purpose for my salvation."[9] Believers may be confident that God sustains the world and everything in it — that is, the realms explored by the academic disciplines — because by faith in Christ they experience the sometimes unfathomable but always beneficial rule of God in every aspect of their own lives.

The academic payoff for this confidence in providence is the conclusion that, if God rules all things with respect to the individual's salvation, certainly he rules as well the more general events and circumstances of the wider world. And this fact must be true even if (as usually happens) we cannot see clearly the mechanisms of that control. In sum, to believe that we are attached to Christ inspires the confidence that God can be attached to anything we might study.

"The Word Was Made Flesh": The Materiality of the Incarnation

More directly related to the person and work of Christ, believers may be greatly heartened in studying the material world and the physical qualities of human existence by reflecting on the material character of the incarnation. The great expression of this reality is the passage in John 1 that we have already quoted: "The Word became flesh and made his dwelling among us. We have seen his glory, the glory of the One and Only, who came from the Father, full of grace and truth" (1:14). Theologian Michael Williams has provided the sort of gloss on

---

9. *Creeds and Confessions,* 2:429.

this passage that properly deflates the dangerous tendency to overspiritualize an understanding of God's work in the world: "John 1:14 does not say that the Word became *nous* [mind]. It says that the Word became *sarx* [flesh] — the bodily stuff of God's good creation. The Word became flesh not in some abstract realm of truth where only minds exist, but in history. . . . Dwelling among us, he was seen by flesh and blood, particular human beings. Pretty material stuff. Pretty historical. Glorious."[10]

Robert Barron has extended this acute reflection by showing how trust in the incarnate Christ protects against the extreme Platonism that Williams warns against, but also against the more modern sundering of matter and mind. First is the Christian truth: "The Word — the rational truth in all of its forms — manifests itself in the vagaries and particularities of history and is received according to the capacity and complexity of an embodied mind." Then the intellectual application: proper knowledge arises "neither through escape from the body (Platonism) nor sequestration of the mind from the body (modern Cartesianism and Lockeanism), but through a rough, incarnate interaction of matter and spirit."[11]

The Southern Baptist educator William Hull stressed how the materiality of the incarnation is to be appropriated: "Flesh for God is not a mask, a disguise, or a subterfuge as the Gnostics supposed. Rather, it is a strategy, a witness, a vehicle for involvement. God's Son wants high visibility in order to be seen and heard and touched by others."[12]

If it is true that the Word became flesh, it must also be true that the realm that bore the Word, the realm of flesh, is worthy of the most serious consideration. Believers will never study the material world as if it were the only realm or necessarily the most basic realm. But to know that the material world is the realm in which God revealed himself most fully should be sufficient reason to study that realm with

10. Michael Williams, review of *The Word Became Flesh*, by Millard Erickson, *Pro Rege*, September 1992, 27.

11. Barron, *The Priority of Christ*, 182.

12. William W. Hull, "We Would See Jesus" (sermon on John 12:21), *Occasional Papers of the Provost*, Samford University (February 12, 1995), 10.

great, if not ultimate, seriousness. In sum, to confess the material reality of the incarnation is to perceive an unusual dignity in the material world itself.

"You Have Saved the Best Till Now": The This-Worldliness of the Incarnation

By a similar logic, the this-worldly character of the incarnation can lead to a particularly Christian delight in creative human engagement with the terrestrial realm. That is, the reality of Christ points, not simply to an engagement with the world, but to an engagement marked by delight, exuberance, and the aesthetic possibility of redemption. At the foundation of Christian self-definition is the process described in the fourth chapter of Galatians: "When the time had fully come, God sent his Son, born of a woman, born under law, to redeem those under law, that we might receive the full rights of sons" (vv. 4-5). The full rights of son- and daughter-ship certainly must include the opportunity to take pleasure in what God is and what he has done.

At the marriage feast of Cana, to which we have already alluded, Jesus turned water into wine of such quality that the banquet host was startled. Instead of serving the best wine at the start of the feast, Jesus' astonishing act took place after the initial beverage supply had run out. Yet when the newly created wine was served, the emcee marveled that "you have saved the best till now" (John 2:10). The depiction of Jesus' actions at this wedding feast does not square easily with later Christian tendencies to extreme asceticism, or even with hyper-pious squeamishness about taking a drink — though of course at other points in his life Jesus also modeled ascetic self-discipline as well. More important even than the action itself, however, are John's words about the action's significance. Turning water into wine was Jesus' first public "sign" (RSV) or "miraculous sign" (NIV); it was an action that allowed his glory to be revealed; and it led his followers to "put their faith in him" (John 2:11).

The accomplishment of redemption *in* this world, more even

than the fact of divine incarnation in this world, is what gives Christian engagement with the world the potential of delight. The Polish poet Czeslaw Milosz, even after living under the worst that Stalinist colonialism could offer, did not lose his wonder at the marvels of redemption. He expressed that wonder once in a poem that began with a premise: "If God incarnated himself in man, died and rose from the dead," for which he then supplied the consequence: "All human endeavors deserve attention / Only to the degree that they depend on this." The result of the incarnation was to see "how human history is holy" and to realize that because in the incarnation "our kind was so much elevated," all people now had an opportunity to "testify to the divine glory / With words, music, dance, and every sign."[13]

The historian Richard Jenkyns has remarked on the potential exuberance of Christian engagement in the world by comparing that engagement with an ancient Greek way:

> Platonism imposes a paradox: the beauties of the perceptible world are merely imperfect imitations of the eternal beauty of the world of forms. In a way this devalues the world known to our senses, but in another way it exalts it, for the perceptible world is indeed beautiful — that is not denied — and it is also our means of access to a higher and unchanging beauty. Christianity presents a similar paradox: this world may be of less account than the one to come, but that does not make it unimportant; it is, indeed, the theater in which the great drama of salvation and damnation is to be played out.[14]

In sum, to confess that the people of God have been redeemed by the action of God *in this world* is to bestow the potential of drama and delight on human engagement with the world.

---

13. Czeslaw Milosz, "Either-Or," in *New and Collected Poems (1931-2001)* (New York: Ecco, 2001), 540.

14. Jenkyns, "The Bellow and the Uproar," review of *Flesh and Stone: The Body and the City in Western Civilization,* by R. Sennett, *New York Review,* March 2, 1995, 32.

"Who Do People Say That the Son of Man Is?": The Personality of the Incarnation

The sixteenth chapter of the Gospel of Matthew records a question, posed by Jesus to his disciples, that has been asked time and again in all ages and in every place to which the Christian message comes: "Who do people say the Son of Man is?" (Matt. 16:13). Peter's answer has been definitive for all Christian traditions: "You are the Christ [i.e., Messiah, God's anointed one], the Son of the living God" (Matt. 16:16). Traditionally, Christian believers have pointed to what this passage signifies for the meaning of the incarnation, the fact of God becoming human. But in recent decades, a number of Christian thinkers have wanted to say more. If Jesus Christ shows us God in human flesh, does not God-in-human-flesh also show us something of great importance about humanity? This emphasis has been especially prominent among Roman Catholic theologians.

Both Pope John Paul II and Pope Benedict XVI have referred frequently to statements in the Second Vatican Council's "Pastoral Constitution on the Church in the Modern World" *(Gaudium et Spes)* as they describe the meaning of Christ for understanding human nature. As the incarnate Son, "He worked with human hands, He thought with a human mind, acted by a human choice, and loved with a human heart. Born of the Virgin Mary, He has truly been made one of us, like us in all things except sin." The consequence of Christ's full identification with humanity as a human himself is that "only in the mystery of the incarnate Word does the mystery of man take on light. For Adam, the first man, was a figure of Him who was to come, namely, Christ the Lord. Christ, the final Adam, by the revelation of the mystery of the Father and His love, fully reveals man to man himself and makes his supreme calling clear."[15] A later Catholic author has summarized the prominent strand of Christian personalism

15. *The Documents of Vatican II,* ed. Walter M. Abbott, S.J. (New York: Guild Press, 1966), 221, 220 (par. 22 of *Gaudium et Spes*). For learned commentary on John Paul II's development of these themes, see George H. Williams, *The Mind of John Paul II* (New York: Seabury Press, 1981), 265-66.

grounded in the Council's statements: "God so esteems man as to assume his humanity and give Himself up to death for him."[16]

The importance of such reflections for scholarship is to dignify human study of human beings. Put differently, the *personality* of the incarnation justifies the study of human personality. When people examine other people, they are examining individuals who exist in actual or potential solidarity with Jesus Christ. Further insight from Christian teaching is necessary to explain the full meaning of that solidarity. But the solidarity itself offers a powerful Christian resource for taking up serious study of the human person and the human personality.

"His Face Shone Like the Sun": The Beauty of the Incarnate Son

In the seventeenth chapter of Matthew appears the story of Jesus' transfiguration. Just before relating this story, the Gospel records that "Jesus began to explain to his disciples that he must go to Jerusalem and suffer many things at the hands of the elders, chief priests and teachers of the law, and that he must be killed and on the third day be raised to life" (Matt. 16:21). Then Jesus spoke words about the need for his followers to suffer (16:25) and about the relative unimportance of "the whole world" compared to the much more important matter of eternal life. This is the context for the account of Jesus taking three of his disciples onto a high mountain where "he was transfigured before them. His face shone like the sun, and his clothes became as white as the light" (17:2). As this startling transformation occurs the three disciples see two other figures — Moses, the great lawgiver, and Elijah, the prophet of righteousness — talking with the transfigured Christ. Peter proposes making some kind of memorial to commemorate this great event, but he is roughly broken off when "a bright cloud" overwhelms all of them and a voice comes from the cloud to

16. Thomas D. Williams, L.C., *Who Is My Neighbor? Personalism and the Foundation of Human Rights* (Washington, DC: Catholic University of America Press, 2005), 215.

say: "This is my Son, whom I love; with him I am well pleased. Listen to him!" (17:5). The disciples fall to the ground, overcome with awe, but then Jesus comes to them, touches them, urges them to rise, and — most remarkably — tells them, "Don't be afraid" (17:7).

The primary meaning of this passage must surely be its singling out of Christ as the one to whom the great code of divine law (Moses) and the great work of prophetic revelation (Elijah) pointed as their fulfillment. That meaning has been the subject of a modern hymn by Carl Daw, which catches succinctly the burden of the passage as bringing to culmination several prominent themes of Old Testament revelation. Along the way, however, Daw's hymn also makes a strong aesthetic statement:

> Light breaks through our clouds and shadows,
> splendor bathes the flesh-joined Word;
> Moses and Elijah marvel
> as the heavenly voice is heard.
> Eyes and hearts behold with wonder
> how the Law and Prophets meet:
> Christ with garments drenched in brightness,
> stands transfigured and complete.[17]

The aesthetic bearing of the hymn concerns Christ as "light" and "splendor" with "garments drenched in brightness." The one who brings the law and prophets to completion is a being of unimaginable beauty. When the qualities of deity are unveiled, Jesus Christ appears in brilliant light. This is the one who will suffer and die for his people. The God who dwells in unapproachable glory has appeared in Jesus Christ, who as an ordinary human being is nonetheless a being of surpassing beauty.

Aesthetically this depiction of Christ suggests that he is the summit of all that is beautiful. Where proportion, harmony, fittingness, excellence, and balance exist in this world, they reflect in human measure what appeared on the Mount of Transfiguration without reserve.

17. Carl P. Daw, "We Have Come at Christ's Own Bidding," *Worship and Praise* (Carol Stream, IL: Hope Publishing, 2001), no. 245.

The centrality of Christ for aesthetics was intimated powerfully in the writings of Jonathan Edwards, whose theological meditations have echoed far from his setting in western Massachusetts at the middle of the eighteenth century. What Edwards had to say on related questions repays attention from those who would try to explain the ineffable with mere words. Near the end of his life — as, in effect, a summation of four decades of intense theological reflection — Edwards wrote *Two Dissertations: Concerning the End for Which God Created the World* [and] *The Nature of True Virtue* (published posthumously in 1765). In these coordinated dissertations, Edwards combined biblical and ethical reflections on the being and actions of God considered in themselves, along with the dispositions of human life considered in relationship to God. Conceptions of beauty played a large part in Edwards's description of God as the supreme being: "For as God is infinitely the greatest being, so he is allowed to be infinitely the most beautiful and excellent: and all the beauty to be found throughout the whole creation is but the reflection of the diffused beams of that Being who hath an infinite fullness of brightness and glory."[18] The link to the person of Christ was the glory that burst forth on the Mount of Transfiguration: "On the whole," wrote Edwards, "it is pretty manifest that Jesus Christ sought the glory of God as his highest and last end; and that therefore . . . this was God's last end in the creation of the world."[19]

The chain of reasoning prompted by Edwards's reflections cannot function as an airtight proof to guide second-order considerations of beauty. It can, however, indicate how the revelation of divine glory in Jesus Christ — as singularly displayed on the Mount of Transfiguration — might frame thinking about first-order aesthetic experiences. In sum, the beauties of creation reflect the fullness of the being of God; the person of Jesus Christ is God incarnate in human flesh; through learning of Jesus Christ we learn of God's chief purpose in creating the world; that chief purpose is the manifestation of his own

18. Jonathan Edwards, *Two Dissertations: The Nature of True Virtue,* ed. Paul Ramsey, in *The Works of Jonathan Edwards,* vol. 8 (New Haven: Yale University Press, 1989), 550-51.

19. Edwards, *Two Dissertations: Concerning the End for Which God Created the World,* in *The Works of Jonathan Edwards,* 8:484.

glory; the manifestation of God's glory accounts for the deep origin of all that is beautiful in the world.

* * *

The Christian religion embodies a narrative that can be summarized simply, however profound the implications and however controversial those implications have become. God made the world and everything in it; God revealed himself in a particular manner to Abraham and his descendants (Israel); the culmination of God's revelation to Israel, and through Israel to all humankind, was the incarnation of Jesus Christ as a full human being; Jesus was born miraculously, he lived a perfect life, he was executed, he was raised from the dead; as he ascended into heaven, the resurrected Christ commissioned the Holy Spirit to continue his redemptive work in the world; at the end of time the triune God will renew the work accomplished in Jesus Christ through the restoration of all things. The primary purpose of this Christian story is (as an echo of Jonathan Edwards) for God through Christ to reconcile sinful human beings to himself, and all for the praise of his own glory.

But if redemption of humans for the glory of God is the great purpose of the Christian story, that overriding telos encompasses many other purposes. Because of a series of contingent events over the last two centuries, it has become conventional to think that belief in the Christian story opposes serious commitment to intellectual explorations of the world. There are no good reasons for this opinion. It rests on misreadings of the Christian story and misapprehensions of the intellectual life. The Jesus Christ who saves sinners is the same Christ who beckons his followers to serious use of their minds for serious explorations of the world. It is part of the deepest foundation of Christian reality — it is an important part of understanding who Jesus is and what he accomplishes — to study the world, the human structures found in the world, the human experiences of the world, and the humans who experience the world. Nothing intrinsic in that study should drive a person away from Jesus Christ. Much that is intrinsic in Jesus Christ should drive a person to that study.

THREE

Jesus Christ: Guidance for Serious Learning

—◦◦◦—

G eneral admonitions are, of course, quite different from specific guidelines. If for believers the door to learning is opened wide by Jesus Christ, that fact by itself does not provide detailed directions for those who pass through the doorway. The children in C. S. Lewis's stories who went into the land of Narnia were often befuddled, lost, and confused even on that other side of the wardrobe. To say that "all things" have been made by the Son of God and now "hold together" in him can remain hollow triumphalism unless it is shown that such affirmations make a difference in concrete practice. As difficult as it may seem to reorient thinking toward the "treasures of wisdom and knowledge" found in Jesus Christ, it can be just as difficult to move past slogans and actually carry out real intellectual activity.

It is foolish to underestimate the barriers standing in the way of a christological approach to study. Apart from the work of some philosophers, serious academic research guided by explicit Christian norms has been thin on the ground for at least two hundred years. To be sure, the sterling record of luminaries from the heights of European Christian civilization — from Anselm and Aquinas to Boyle, Pascal, Bach, Edwards, and Malebranche — provides remarkable historical precedent for Christian intellectuals today who want to walk where these forerunners ran. But for at least the last two centuries the drift has been the other way — for first-order research and compelling arguments to be defined by a values-neutral conception of truth and energized by liberation from dogma.

Resources, however, are abundant for trying to advance scholarship on a Christian foundation. For instance, the claim that modern science, ethics, aesthetics, history, social science, psychiatry, and even criticism rest on a presumed or submerged theism deserves much more consideration than it regularly receives. The issue specifically is whether there is any good reason, apart from an active deity, to take for granted the regularity, communicability, universality, durability, and repeatability that are so basic for so many intellectual endeavors. But even that significant contextual assertion has been advanced only rarely by Christian thinkers in the modern marketplace of ideas. The much more obvious reality is that scientists, philosophers, historians, and critics have long been acting as if general theistic considerations, much less explicitly Christian concerns, were irrelevant.

The result is that even basic intellectual moves can pose difficulties. In my own case I have been thinking about the bearing of Christology on historical practice for more than a quarter century and am not at all certain that I have cracked this particular nut successfully. Nonetheless, as a stimulus for others who are expert in the various disciplines of modern learning and who would like to explore the call of Christ in their labors, this chapter and the four that follow try to suggest specific ways that the teaching of the creeds might make an intellectual difference. Although this effort means rushing in where angels fear to tread, it may still indicate live possibilities in Christian orthodoxy for orientations, dispositions, attitudes, or preferences in carrying out specific intellectual tasks.

In this chapter the focus is on four general expectations that might inform intellectual life if the grand claims of John 1, Colossians 1, and Hebrews 1 are taken seriously, and if the formulations in the major creeds could function as guides to understanding the world. The four concern duality or doubleness, contingency, particularity, and self-denial. Care is required to spell out how such stances derive from basic orthodox Christology and how they can guide expectations for learning — perhaps more care than I can provide. Yet once the nature of Christ's person and work is grasped, and then the centrality of Christ for all things, these four stances should seem noncontroversial.

I offer specific suggestions about the actual workings of several academic disciplines in the next chapters, but my aim is not pontification but stimulation. These chapters are not pretending to lay down laws for Christian intellectual life but are trying to show that such life can arise as a natural extension of Christian belief itself.

Doubleness

The expectation that some important results of scholarship will have a dual or doubled character would seem to flow naturally from the realities summarized by the Chalcedonian Definition. Those realities point to a paradox or an apparent antinomy in the most basic understanding of the Christian faith. It would then seem to follow, if "all things" exist from, in, and for Christ, that the dual nature of Christ would give shape to at least some of what humans grasp in their efforts to understand existence in general.

The crucial phrases from Chalcedon affirm a particular two-in-one-ness about the Lord whom Christians have always trusted as the bedrock of their existence. Specifically, the incarnate Son of God was "one and the same Christ, Son, Lord, Only-begotten, acknowledged in two natures which undergo no confusion, no change, no division, no separation; at no point was the difference between the natures taken away through the union, but rather the property of both natures is preserved and comes together into a single person and a single subsistent being; he is not parted or divided into two persons, but is one and the same only-begotten Son, God, Word, Lord Jesus Christ."[1] Christianity in its entirety is a religion grounded in what Chalcedon tried to describe: Jesus Christ accomplished his mediatorial work because he was both divine and human — moreover, divine and human joined in one integrated person without confusion, change, division, or separation.

1. *Creeds and Confessions of Faith in the Christian Tradition,* ed. Jaroslav Pelikan and Valerie Hotchkiss, 3 vols. (New Haven: Yale University Press, 2003), 1:181.

Even though ordinary human wisdom declares that divinity and humanity cannot be conjoined as Chalcedon affirms they were, Christ was and is a being with two natures in one integrated person. All the orthodox Christian traditions are based on this foundational truth instead of ordinary human wisdom. Believers, therefore, have every reason to expect breakthroughs in scholarship, insofar as they allow crucial christological convictions to guide their scholarly perspectives.

The transition from inward faith resting on christological affirmation to outward study informed by christological reality can be simply stated, even if it is difficult to execute: the doubleness of Christ as divine and human, which undergirds the whole edifice of Christian life and thought, is a model for studying the spheres of existence.

Christian scholars who take to heart Chalcedonian doctrine about the divine and human present in one integrated Person should be predisposed to seek knowledge about particular matters from more than one angle. The wisdom of that expectation is underscored by frequent illustrations in Scripture.

> Acts 2:23: "This man was handed over to you by God's set purpose and foreknowledge; and you, with the help of wicked men, put him to death by nailing him to the cross."

> Nehemiah 2:8 (and parallels in Ezra 7:6, 9): "And because the gracious hand of my God was upon me, the king granted my requests."

> Psalm 77:19: "Your path led through the sea, / your way through the mighty waters, / though your footprints were not seen."

These instances show the biblical authors recognizing multiple legitimate skeins of cause and effect to explain single human actions. One lies in the purposes of God; others in the realm of ordinary human activity. They are models to be taken seriously, not as if humans can have God-like understanding, but that they too can approach reality with Chalcedonian expectations.

The way four theologians have written about this perspective suggests what a Christ-centered angle of vision might entail for learned exploration of academic subjects. First is an assertion in the famous prayer of Anselm of Canterbury at the start of his *Proslogion,* the work from the late eleventh century that tried to demonstrate the existence of God by what would later be called the ontological argument. In this prayer, Anselm enacted a common Christian pattern by basing what he knew on what he had experienced: "I do not attempt, O Lord, to penetrate Thy profundity, for I desire to understand in some degree Thy truth, which my heart believes and loves. For I do not seek to understand, in order that I may believe; but I believe that I may understand. For I believe this too, that unless I believed, I should not understand."[2] What Anselm in his heart believed and loved was clearly the Savior Jesus Christ, the nature of whose sacrifice on behalf of sinners he had also explored in a famous treatise on the atonement, *Cur Deus Homo?* (Why did God become human?) In other words, Anselm's contemplation of philosophical proof for the existence of God proceeded from his faith in Christ.

A second theologian expanding upon this same vision was Benjamin Breckinridge Warfield, the conservative Presbyterian who at the end of the nineteenth century reiterated the crucial standing of creedal affirmations for all of Christian life. In Warfield's view, the life of Christ "everywhere" reveals "a double life unveiled before us in the dramatization of the actions of Jesus. . . . [A] double life is attributed to him as his constant possession." Warfield readily acknowledged that "this conjoint humanity and deity, within the limits of a single personality, presents serious problems to the human intellect, in its attempts to comprehend it, in itself or in its activities." But despite these difficulties, Warfield proclaimed that "we cannot afford to lose either the God in the man or the man in the God; our hearts cry out for the complete God-man whom the Scriptures offer us." Christianity in its entirety hung upon this biblical picture: "Because he is man he is able to pour out his blood, and because he is God his blood is of infinite value to save . . . it is only because he is both God and Man in one person, that we can speak of God purchasing his Church with his own

2. Anselm, *Proslogion,* quoted in Frederick Copleston, *A History of Philosophy,* vol. 2 (Garden City, NY: Image, 1962), 177.

blood. . . . And unless God has purchased his Church with his own blood, in what shall his Church find a ground for its hope?"[3] In the essay containing these considerations, Warfield did not apply his reasoning to other issues. But as we will see in later chapters, his sense of the doubleness of the incarnation proved very important as he approached controversial questions in science and for the study of Scripture itself.[4]

More recently, Gabriel Fackre has noted the tendency in Christian history for believers to shy away from what he calls the "antinomies all over scripture and Christian teaching, paradigmatically in the doctrine of the incarnation." The reason, claims Fackre, is that "the assertion of mutually exclusive propositions — humanity and divinity in one person — never satisfies human reason, which is always interested in relaxing the tension in one direction or the other."[5] Like Warfield, Fackre did not go on to make applications for scholarship in general from his theological point, but the applications would seem to flow naturally: If the center of human history has the character he described, why not at least some of the peripheries?

A final statement comes from an essay by Robert Palma on connections between Michael Polanyi's conceptions of scientific practice and "christological dualisms." According to Palma, who examined several of the seeming tensions in twentieth-century conceptions of Christ (for example, the Christ of faith versus the Jesus of history), "such valid dualities did not function as dichotomies or divisions" for the early Christian fathers. Rather, the authors of the creeds felt that such dualities were "bound up together personally through God's own life and [could be] viewed as components of a divinely constituted historic and coherent gestalt of grace."[6] Palma suggested that Polanyi's

---

3. B. B. Warfield, "The Human Development of Jesus," in *The Bible Student,* vol. 1 (1900), 12-19; quoted here from *Selected Shorter Writings,* vol. 1, ed. John E. Meeter (Phillipsburg, NJ: Presbyterian and Reformed, 1970), 163, 164, 166.

4. See below, 110-16 and 130-32.

5. Gabriel Fackre, "An Evangelical Megashift?" *Christian Century,* May 3, 1995, 485.

6. Robert J. Palma, "Polanyi and Christological Dualisms," *Scottish Journal of Theology* 48 (1995): 212.

approach to science, which describes it as simultaneously objective conclusions about nature and human practices aimed at understanding nature, illustrates how approaches to thought from the early Christian centuries might lead to another kind of gestalt for modern interpreters who confront apparently irreconcilable dichotomies.

Where Christian scholars might go in their scholarship, if Chalcedon were fixed centrally in their minds, depends very much upon individual disciplines and specific problems. Engineering, some forms of math, and some aspects of musical theory might not be different in Chalcedonian perspective. But a Chalcedonian orientation might make a difference in contemporary epistemology that puts point of view into conflict with information coming from outside the self; in basic physics with investigations of light as waves or particles; in historical interpretations that find two or more plausible explanations for the same event; in theories of human behavior stressing sometimes free choice and sometimes determined action; or in biology confronted with the randomness of evolutionary change and the complexity of advanced organisms. The natural human urge moves to adjudicate competition among overarching claims. This urge, which relies on the practical necessity of the law of noncontradiction, must certainly be trusted in many specific scholarly arenas. But for a Christian who has experienced the saving power of Christ, it will be a smaller step, when confronting at least some dichotomous intellectual problems, to seek the harmonious acceptance of the dichotomy than for a scholar who does not believe that the integrated person of Christ was made up of a fully divine and a fully human nature.

Contingency

Traditional Christianity involves a central place for contingency because of the biblical accounts that describe how earnest seekers found Christ or proclaimed Christ. Although a full definition of contingency would involve heavy philosophical slogging, a simpler definition is adequate here. Contingent statements are those that are neither necessarily true ($2 + 2 = 4$) nor necessarily false (ordinary sheep have five legs). Contingency in general means that something is the way it is, not because it has to be that way, but because it developed or worked out the way it did. For intellectual purposes, contingency means that if we want to find out about the workings of nature, the reasons why historical events took place and historical circumstances existed, or the motives behind human actions in the present or the past, we must not simply reason downward from philosophical or theological convictions, but must seek out as much evidence as possible about whatever we are studying.

Contingency in this basic sense frames the search for God as described in the Old Testament, especially in the Psalms. Thus, God is known in his works of creation as humans heed what nature communicates:

> The heavens declare the glory of God;
>   the skies proclaim the work of his hands.
> Day after day they pour forth speech;
>   night after night they display knowledge.
> There is no speech or language
>   where their voice is not heard.
> Their voice goes out into all the earth,
>   their words to the ends of the world.
>
> (19:1-4)

After relating the deliverance he had experienced by God's mercy, another psalmist urges women and men to "taste and see that the LORD is good" (34:8). And the well-known prayer of Psalm 119 is that God would

> Open my eyes that I may see
>   wonderful things in your law.
>
> (119:18)

In the New Testament, the message of the apostles did not primarily concern necessary truths of reason, but rather truths hard-won through experience. Peter and John explained their boldness in addressing Jerusalem's religious rulers about Christ by saying, "we cannot help speaking about what we have seen and heard" (Acts 4:20). And the apostle Paul told one of his Roman interrogators that the way Christ directed Paul's life course had not escaped the official's notice "because it was not done in a corner" (Acts 26:26). The author to the book of Hebrews urged believers who could not make out the promised rule of God over all things to take heart, because "we see Jesus, who was made a little lower than the angels, now crowned with glory and honor because he suffered death, so that by the grace of God he might taste death for everyone" (Heb. 2:9). Confidence in the promise unseen, in other words, rested on what had been seen. The First Epistle of John offers the same reliance on firsthand experience as the basis for believing the Christian message: "That which was from the beginning, which we have heard, which we have seen with our eyes, which we have looked at and our hands have touched — this we proclaim concerning the Word of Life. . . . We proclaim to you what we have seen and heard" (1 John 1:1, 3).

In such proclamations, the apostolic authors were only following the lead of the Gospels. The Gospel of John records that after Philip had encountered Jesus, Philip told his friend Nathanael he had "found the one Moses wrote about in the Law, and about whom the prophets also wrote — Jesus of Nazareth." But Nathanael simply knew that God's promised one could not come from Nazareth, to which Philip offered this assured reply: "Come and see" (John 1:45, 46). The Samaritan woman who met Jesus at the well in Sychar likewise urged her fellow citizens to put aside their prejudice against Jewish teachers and "Come, see a man who told me everything I ever did. Could this be the Christ?" (John 4:29). Jesus, memorably, responded in the same way to the disciples of John when they came asking on behalf of their imprisoned leader if Jesus was "the one who was to come, or should we expect someone else?" The reply was to tell John "what you hear and see: The blind receive sight, the lame walk, those who have leprosy are cured, the deaf hear, the dead are raised, and the good news is preached to the poor" (Matt. 11:3, 4-5). In these scriptural cases, the evidence of experience was to guide thinking; mental dispositions, while not unimportant, were not most important.

The specific christological implication of these passages concerns the surface implausibility of an incarnate deity and the further implausibility of a hope for human salvation arising from such an incarnation. To all forms of unbelief, however, the response is the same: come and see.[7] For any number of reasons, Christian realities do not make sense, until and unless they have been experienced. They are in that sense contingent realities.

The contingency of the incarnation and the work of Christ would seem to justify a related commitment to empirical procedures as a way of learning about the world. If we come to know God best by correcting our prejudgments about what God can or cannot do through experiencing what God has actually done, it follows that we learn about the world by opening up our prejudgments about what we think the world must be like to how we actually experience the world. The principle is that if we want to know something, we must not only think about that something, but actually experience it. God may be able to think his way to reality, but we cannot. If we know God by experiencing him, so also do we come to know the world.

A preference for empirical over deductive reasoning can never be absolute, but it is a reliable preference that allows for an escape from pure constructionism (the assertion that reports of "experiences" are simply coded statements about our own social, political, or gender locations). A reliance on sense experience for genuine insights is too well established in too many biblical texts. Even more valuable, it allows for an escape from deductive dogmatism. A sobering example of such dogmatism from recent American history is the Vietnam War. Because key national leaders held the general belief that communism was a monolithic ideology controlled by the Soviet Union and aimed systematically at world domination, there seemed no need

---

7. David Hume's famous argument that the experience of ordinary human life trumps every claim to have experienced the supernatural has been thoughtfully treated in several recent works. For a sympathetic interpretation of Hume with the relevant texts, see Robert J. Fogelin, *A Defense of Hume on Miracles* (Princeton: Princeton University Press, 2003). Treatments that find serious weaknesses in Hume's arguments include David Johnson, *Hume, Holism, and Miracles* (Ithaca, NY: Cornell University Press, 1999), and John Earman, *Hume's Abject Failure: The Argument against Miracles* (New York: Oxford University Press, 2000).

for close study of what was actually happening in Southeast Asia. Inductive experience about the actual situation on the ground in Vietnam was less important for policy makers than what they simply knew must be the case about communism in general. The result of such thinking was military and diplomatic disaster.

Examples abound of similar instances, with classic standoffs on scientific questions probably foremost. Some individuals who properly trust the revelation of Scripture simply know that, since God created everything, evolution cannot be true — and so there is no need to carefully gather and weigh evidence about how the world actually works. Other individuals who properly trust the evidence of their senses when exploring nature conclude that evolution works randomly, and since they simply know that randomness excludes divine providence, God cannot superintend nature — and so there is no need to carefully gather evidence about how the existence of divinity and the existence of a material world might be related.

More such deductive dogmatisms will be explored in later chapters, but here it is enough to conclude with testimony by Christian thinkers from several venues who felt it was a Christian duty to pursue the way of empiricism. Thus, the eighteenth-century poet Christopher Smart once wrote about how best to honor the Scriptures as God's written revelation. The way to go was not reasoning downward from what one knew the Bible must be, but reasoning upward as one actually read it:

> O take the book from off the shelf,
>   And con it meekly on thy knees;
> Best panegyric on itself,
>   And self avouched to teach and please.[8]

The great theologian and New Testament scholar Adolf Schlatter battled throughout his career in late-nineteenth- and early-twentieth-century Germany to defend orthodox and pietistic interpretations of the faith. Once in writing on the mistakes of atheism, he paused to

---

8. Smart, quoted from *The Poet's Book of Psalms,* ed. Laurance Wieder (New York: Harper Collins, 1995), xvi.

53

recommend the intellectual method that he felt best reflected the character of the universe as God had made it: "What obligates as members of the *universitas litterarum* [scholarly guild] as an inviolable duty is that we, in the field of labor appointed to us, succeed at seeing, at chaste, unsullied observation, at a comprehension of the real event, be it one that took place in the past or one that is just now happening." Schlatter felt that "every labor within the university" demanded that same perspective. He concluded by stating boldly that "Science is first seeing and secondly seeing and thirdly seeing and again and again seeing. . . . Therefore it is a general and inviolable scientific rule that every judgment must be preceded by painstaking observation, and all our own conclusions must be preceded by the act of reception, without which our own production bursts into wind and illusions."[9] For Schlatter this was the way not just of academic respectability but also of Christian integrity.

During World War II the archbishop of Canterbury, William Temple, recommended a similar empirical approach as the best strategy for churches to handle social or political issues. In particular, he thought that churches should not pontificate on "any particular policy," since experience in the world was the crucial element in adopting any specific way ahead: "A policy always depends on technical decisions concerning the actual relations of cause and effect in the political and economic world; about these a Christian as such has no more reliable judgment than an atheist, except so far as he should be more immune to the temptations of self-interest."[10] Temple did not mean that Christian principles or truth claims were unimportant; he did mean that knowledge of a particular situation gained by experience with that particular situation was critical for determining the best public policies.

Even more recently, C. Everett Koop complained about the rush

9. "Adolf Schlatter on Atheistic Methods in Theology," trans. David R. Bauer (from 1905), in appendix to Werner Neuer, *Adolf Schlatter: A Biography of Germany's Premier Biblical Theologian,* trans. Robert W. Yarbrough (Grand Rapids: Baker, 1996), 218-20.

10. William Temple, *Christianity and the Social Order* (New York: Seabury Press, 1977; original 1942), 40.

of conclusions before facts that bedeviled his tenure in the 1980s as surgeon general of the United States. Early in that tenure Koop was blasted from the left for his strong personal stance against abortion on demand. But later he came under fire from the right for insisting on humane treatment for those who suffered from HIV/AIDS. His comments about this bombarding amounted to an appeal for patient contingency appropriate for this book: "What bothered me most . . . was the lack of scholarship by Christians — as if they felt that by leaning on a theological principle they didn't have to be very accurate with the facts. People talk about knee-jerk liberals. The liberals have no corner on that market; I've learned there are also knee-jerk conservatives."[11]

Contingency in academic practice reflects the pattern by which God made himself known to earnest seekers in the Old Testament and to the followers of Jesus in the New. It provides an especially strong counter to the tendency of academics to trust their own conclusions instead of letting their ideas be challenged by contact with the world beyond their own minds.

Particularity

One of the most helpful guides for scholarship from classical Christology comes from reflecting on what it means that Jesus was born as the Savior of the world to the Virgin Mary in Bethlehem during the days of Herod, king of Judea. In the Christian scheme of things, this very particular event carries universal meaning for all people at all times and in all places. The implication can be stated succinctly: because God revealed himself most clearly in a particular set of circumstances and at a particular time and place, every other particular set of cultural circumstances takes on a fresh potential importance. The payoff for intellectual life is to provide mediation between the one and the many, the specific and the general, the perspectival and the universal.

Biblical religion offers numerous reasons for paying full atten-

---

11. Koop, quoted in Philip Yancey, *Soul Survivor: How Thirteen Unlikely Mentors Helped My Faith Survive the Church* (New York: Galilee/Doubleday, 2001), 197.

tion to the specific and for valuing the perspectival. Many accounts in the book of Acts, for instance, point toward the potential value of all local human situations. Thus, as commentators have frequently pointed out, the Day of Pentecost reversed the linguistic disorder caused by the hubris on display at the Tower of Babel (Gen. 11). In that ancient story, diversity of languages led to chaos. But at Pentecost, the Holy Spirit's testimony to the resurrected Christ enabled people of all languages to hear the good news, even as each language retained its own identity: "When they heard this sound [the blowing of a violent wind], a crowd came together in bewilderment, because each one heard them speaking in his own language" (Acts 2:6).

Later in Acts the linguistic diversity of Pentecost is matched by an acceptance of cultural diversity. In chapter 10 the apostle Peter receives repeated divine instructions to set aside Jewish dietary laws in order to communicate the gospel to those who did not observe those laws. Immediately thereafter, when Peter begins his presentation to the Roman centurion Cornelius and his household, he makes a statement with broad cultural, as well as religious, application: "Then Peter began to speak [to Cornelius]: 'I now realize how true it is that God does not show favoritism but accepts men from every nation who fear him and do what is right'" (Acts 10:34-35). While God calls people "from every nation" to repent and turn to him, God also does not play favorites, and so looks on "every nation" as a source of potential good.

The story of the apostle Paul in Athens, related in Acts 17, points in the same direction. Paul has come for the first time to this metropole of Hellenism, where he is struck by the altars erected to various gods. In response he proclaims the message of the one true God who has now manifested himself fully in the person of Jesus Christ and demonstrated the proof of that revelation by raising Christ from the dead. In the course of this exclusionary message, Paul makes a broadly inclusionary statement about the nature of human civilizations: "From one man he made every nation of men, that they should inhabit the whole earth; and he determined the times set for them and the exact places where they should live. God did this so that men would seek him and perhaps reach out for him and find him, though he is not far from each one of us" (Acts 17:26-27). The very diversity of human kinds and cultures speaks not only of God's good creation, but also of his merciful plans for redemption.

Missiologists like Lamin Sanneh and Andrew Walls have seen most clearly how the universal meaning of the incarnation both relativizes and dignifies all other cultural situations. Andrew Walls depicts the tension like this:

> Christ took flesh and was made man in a particular time and place, family, nationality, tradition and customs and sanctified them, while still being for all men in every time and place. Wherever he is taken by the people of any day, time and place, he sanctifies that culture — he is living in it. . . . But to acknowledge this is not to forget that there is another, and equally important, force at work among us. Not only does God in His mercy take people as they are: He takes them to transform them into what He wants them to be.[12]

Sanneh extends the insight to show how Christian particularity is also the basis for exchange among cultures:

> The localization of Christianity is an essential part of the nature of the religion, and . . . without that concrete, historical grounding Christianity becomes nothing but a fragile, elusive abstraction, salt without its saltiness. This is the problem which dogs all attempts at defining the core of the gospel as pure dogmatic system without regard to the concrete lives of men and women who call themselves Christian. And it is precisely the historical concreteness of Christianity which makes cross-cultural mutuality possible and meaningful.[13]

The implications for Christian scholarship from such a double-sided picture of redemption stretch the mind considerably. On the

12. Andrew Walls, "Africa and Christian Identity," in *Mission Focus: Current Issues,* ed. Wilbert R. Shenk (Scottdale, PA: Herald, 1980), 217.

13. Lamin Sanneh, "Gospel and Culture: Ramifying Effects of Scriptural Translation," in *Bible Translation and the Spread of the Church: The Last 200 Years,* ed. Philip C. Stine (Leiden: Brill, 1990), 10-11.

one hand, the particularity at the center of Christianity justifies a rooted, perspectival understanding of truth that embraces unabashedly the crucial significance of all other particularities of time, place, cultural value, and social location. On the other hand, since the birth of Christ was for all people in all times and places, the incarnation undergirds confidence in the possibility of universal truth. Christian support for theories of culture based on the particularity of social expression is, therefore, very strong. But that support does not verge over into nihilism or a relativism denying the presence of universal value. The key is that God used the particular means of the incarnation to accomplish a universal redemption.

With this understanding, believers can negotiate calmly through the perilous tides of modernity and postmodernity. On the one side, the once-for-all character of the incarnation of God in Christ establishes the universality of truth as vigorously as did the most ardent advocates of the Enlightenment. But on the other side, the incarnation represented a divinely constituted particularity and so affirms the perspectival character of truth as radically as the postmodernists. Believers in the biblical religion defined by classical doctrines about Christ can, thus, hold together concrete absolutism and nearly infinite flexibility.

What such a conjunction of opposites might mean for studying the particular expressions of culture has only begun to be explored. At the least, however, to confess that the very Son of God who offers salvation to all people everywhere was born during the reign of Augustus Caesar, that he was (in the words of the Apostles' Creed) "crucified under Pontius Pilate," and that he was raised from the dead on the third day — this confession must also affirm the potential value of learning at least something about all other particular cultures in all other times and all other places. The particularity of the Christian story of redemption is meant, first of all, to teach the truth about redemption; but it also communicates a truth about particularity. To confess that Christ experienced a very particular life in first-century Judea and that he is the universal Savior of the world offers a scholar who trusts the Christian story extraordinary intellectual balance when studying other particular lives in other particular places.

The meaning of the category-breaking realities affirmed by orthodox Christology has been put superbly in two poems, one by John Donne at the start of the seventeenth century, the other by G. K. Chesterton at the start of the twentieth. First, John Donne:

> Salvation to all that will is nigh,
> That All, which always is All every where,
> Which cannot sinne, and yet all sinnes must beare,
> Which cannot die, yet cannot chuse but die,
> Loe, faithful Virgin, yeelds himself to lye
> In prison, in thy wombe; and though he there
> Can take no sinne, nor thou give, yet he will weare
> Taken from thence, flesh, which deaths force may trie.
> Ere by the spheares time was created, thou
> Wast in his minde, who is the Sonne, and Brother,
> Whom thou conceiv'st, conceiv'd; yea thou art now
> Thy Makers maker, and thy Fathers mother,
> Thou hast light in darke; and shutst in little roome,
> Immensity cloystered in thy deare wombe.[14]

In Donne's complex metaphysical vision, the antinomies of the incarnation are expressed as the concrete enfleshment of absolutes ("That All, which always is All every where, / . . . yeelds himself to lye / In prison, in thy wombe"; "Ere by the spheares time was created, thou / Wast in his minde [conceiv'd], who is the Sonne, and Brother, / Whom thou conceiv'st"; "Immensity cloystered in thy deare wombe"). It is a vision that stresses both particularity and universality, but — like the incarnation — in one coherent form.

The same combination defines Chesterton's "Gloria in Profundis":

> There has fallen on earth for a token
> A god too great for the sky.
> He has burst out of all things and broken

---

14. John Donne, "Annunciation," in *The Poems of John Donne,* ed. H. J. C. Grierson (Oxford: Clarendon, 1912), 319.

The bounds of eternity:
Into time and the terminal land
He has strayed like a thief or a lover,
For the wine of the world brims over,
Its splendour is spilt on the sand.
. . .
But unmeasured of plummet and rod
Too deep for their sight to scan,
Outrushing the fall of man
Is the height of the fall of God.

Glory to God in the Lowest
The spout of the stars in spate —
Where the thunderbolt thinks to be slowest
And the lightning fears to be late:
As men dive for a sunken gem
Pursuing, we hunt and hound it,
The fallen star that has found it
In the cavern of Bethlehem.[15]

Chesterton is a little lighter, but he appeals for the same response to unfathomable complexity that inspired Donne: this "fall of God" may be "The spout of the stars in spate," and it may be likened to "the thunderbolt" and "the lightning." But the "god too great for the sky" who "has burst out of all things and broken / The bounds of eternity" can only be found by diving, pursuing, hunting, and hounding until it is discovered "In the cavern of Bethlehem."

These poems are trying to express how the universally significant incarnation of the Son of God was also the reality of one very specific local situation — in Donne's case the womb of a single maiden, in Chesterton's the darkness of a single cavern. For Christian believers pursuing the intellectual life, the universal significance of this stark particularity offers a compass for their vocations as well as a light for their lives.

15. G. K. Chesterton, *Gloria in Profundis* (London: Faber and Gwyer, 1927), with wood engraving by Eric Gill.

Self-Denial

Christology also provides a sure antidote to the moral diseases of the intellectual life. As all other God-given gifts and capacities can be turned to evil uses, so also scholarship can be abused to glorify the creature instead of the Creator, to display pride instead of gratitude, and to promote a righteousness of works instead of a righteousness by faith. Even as many believers have practiced scholarship out of gratitude to God, others have found reasons in the intellectual life for giving up Christianity. Yet if gifts from God can be abused, they remain gifts from God. To ensure that the divine gifts that make possible the life of the mind are not wasted or used for idolatry, facts of life as defined by the person and work of Christ are the surest guardian.

The sins of scholars are mostly those common to humankind: the lust of the flesh, the lust of the eyes, and the pride of life. But the predispositions of intellectuals and the circumstances of formal learning also make a few temptations especially threatening. There is pride to be cultivated in degrees earned, books published, honors bestowed, or interviews granted; academic introversion can easily transform into callousness toward people of ordinary intelligence; cliquishness and partisanship can be exploited for promoting my faction, race, sex, or political persuasion at the expense of others; and there is an eagerness to view the gifts that are not congenial to scholarship as somehow less important. These and other sins of intellectuals are familiar to everyone with any experience in the academy. They amount not to an argument against scholarship, but to occasions for redemption. The redemption is found in Christ.

As believing scholars experience that redemption, they realize with full force that they are human and therefore finite. Before the mysteries of the incarnation, intellectuals who realize how much their own work depends on Christ's work simply accept that all intellectual endeavors are limited. Only when, in the words of 1 Corinthians 13, we see Christ "face to face" and are at last "fully known," will Christian believers "know fully." If the mysteries of the incarnation lie beyond full human comprehension, and if Jesus himself confessed during his earthly ministry that there were things he did not know, then scholars following Christ should be doubly aware of how limited their own wisdom truly is. Knowing Christ, in other words, means learning humility.

Applied rightly, Christian intellectual acumen should resonate with passages like Matthew 11 where Jesus describes himself as "gentle and humble in heart" (11:29). It should warn scholars against trying to race ahead of their Savior who "made himself nothing" and took "the very nature of a servant" (Phil. 2:7). It should heed Jesus' blunt word for every servant of God: "So you also, when you have done everything you were told to do, should say, 'We are unworthy servants; we have only done our duty'" (Luke 17:10).

To the extent that scholars are themselves believers, they know that they are sinners who need this Savior. In turn, this knowledge should insulate intellectuals from thinking that any of their own efforts, including intellectual efforts, could do anything to secure their redemption. Put more strongly, a Christ-centered understanding of why all people require an atoning savior demands that scholars not trust their own wisdom as the source of their self-worth. Yet to grasp that scholars are justified by faith and not by their scholarship can also have a tremendously liberating consequence for learning itself. Freed from the delusion that we as scholars can exalt ourselves by our own academic insights, we are therefore freed to serve God joyfully in the academic labors we do attempt. Using God-given mental abilities in gratitude for salvation in Christ is one of the surest ways to avoid thinking that mental abilities bestow special merit.

The tendency to trust in the wrong things has been nicely described by Alice Fryling, who has written about habits all too common among scholars: "We want to impress ourselves and others with all we do and all we can produce. We take God-given gifts, push them beyond their limits and make them sources of pride." When hypocrisy is added to self-delusion, "our lips say that we want to honor God, but the truth may be that we want to show off our gifts or look impressive to others."[16] Such failings are by no means limited to academic are-

---

16. Alice Fryling, *Too Busy? Saying No without Guilt* (Downers Grove, IL: InterVarsity, 2002), 16-17.

nas, but they do constitute standing temptations where intellectual competition is the order of the day.

Christian believers of whatever sort also know that they are members of the church, the body of Christ, where all members share equal dignity and are called to equally important service. Repeated apostolic descriptions explain in detail how the body of Christ needs all its members, whether prominent and publicly praised or little noticed and all but forgotten — not only to function together but to respect one another and work harmoniously with each other. (See, for example, 1 Corinthians 12:12-31.)

In the end, believing scholars are protected from temptation generally, and academic temptations particularly, by the constant awareness that learning is not the most important thing. Significantly, George Herbert's great poem "The Agonie" begins with a reference to what lovers of wisdom ("philosophers") cannot discover on their own, no matter how extensive their learning. Instead Herbert points to the "two vast, spacious things" that enable all believers to approach their callings with gratitude instead of self-congratulation.

> Philosophers have measur'd mountains,
> Fathom'd the depths of seas, of states, and kings,
> Walk'd with a staffe to heav'n, and traced fountains:
>   But there are two vast, spacious things,
> The which to measure it doth more behove:
> Yet few there are that sound them; Sinne and Love.
>
> Who would know Sinne, let him repair
> Unto Mount Olivet; there shall he see
> A man so wrung with pains, that all his hair,
>   His skinne, his garments bloudie be.
> Sinne is that presse and vice, which forceth pain
> To hunt his cruell food through ev'ry vein.
>
> Who knows not Love, let him assay
> And taste that juice, which on the crosse a pike
> Did set again abroach; then let him say
>   If ever he did taste the like.

63

Love is that liquor sweet and most divine,
Which my God feels as bloude; but I, as wine.[17]

*   *   *

Scholarship that is keyed expressly to the person and work of Christ
will not be disoriented by confronting the paradoxical or the mysterious; it will always be more comfortable in what comes to the mind
from outside than in what the mind concludes on its own; it will realize the value of particulars because of Christian universals; and it will
be humble, charitable, self-giving, and modest. The reason in each
case is the same:

> We believe in one God the Father all-powerful, Maker of heaven
> and of earth, and of all things both seen and unseen. And in one
> Lord Jesus Christ, the only-begotten Son of God, begotten from
> the Father before all the ages, light from light, true God from true
> God, begotten not made, consubstantial with the Father, through
> whom all things came to be; for us humans and for our salvation
> he came down from the heavens and became incarnate from the
> Holy Spirit and the Virgin Mary, became human and was crucified
> on our behalf under Pontius Pilate; he suffered and was buried
> and rose up on the third day in accordance with the Scriptures;
> and he went up into the heavens and is seated at the Father's right
> hand; he is coming again with glory to judge the living and the
> dead; his kingdom will have no end.

---

17. "The Agonie," in *The English Poems of George Herbert,* ed. C. A. Patrides (London: Everyman's Library, 1974), 58.

FOUR

The Atonement: A Theological Principle
to Frame Scholarship

—◦◦◦—

R isks accumulate from this point in the book onward. This short chapter tries to show how an evangelical understanding of Christ's saving work might affect scholarship of several kinds. The next chapters move the other way as they consider how study of history, science, and the Bible itself might be undertaken under a christological canopy. All these expositions are self-consciously exploratory. They are not intended as final words laying down a law but as first words urging others to take up the task. Each chapter begins for orientation with an excerpt from one of the classical statements of faith. This one starts where the last chapter ended, by quoting words from the Nicene Creed:

> for us humans and for our salvation he came down from the heavens and became incarnate from the Holy Spirit and the Virgin Mary, became human and was crucified on our behalf under Pontius Pilate; he suffered and was buried and rose up on the third day in accordance with the Scriptures . . .

The experiment in this chapter is to ask a theological principle to serve as a compass for the highways and byways of scholarship. It starts by summarizing a conception of the atonement drawn from the words of the apostle Paul when he affirmed in Colossians 1:20 that Christ made "peace through his blood, shed on the cross." For setting out this particular view of the atonement, I am following the compelling account in John R. W. Stott's 1986 book *The Cross of Christ*,[1] and then trying to push that understanding of the cross toward academic applications. Along the way, many highly relevant questions are bypassed, including issues about theological formation, questions concerning "the new perspective" for understanding Paul on justification, and other vitally consequential matters. I am fully persuaded that others who understand the atonement better than I could do a better job at showing how this foundational Christian reality might shape the pursuits of learning. And I sincerely hope that they may do so.

But for this effort, I begin with Stott's summary of Christ's work of redemption as considered under four heads:[2]

First, *propitiation* (an image from the temple)
Second, *redemption* (an image from the marketplace)
Third, *justification* (an image from the law courts)
Fourth, *reconciliation* (an image from the household)

Propitiation is the theme that requires most explanation in our day since many criticisms have been raised against the idea conveyed by the term, that the cross of Christ turns God's anger away from guilty sinners. A history of revulsion against the notion of God exercising wrath in this way stretches back at least to the medieval scholar Abelard in the twelfth century. Such objections have multiplied in the modern age out of concern for the runaway abuses of power that can be perceived as aping the display of raw power thought to be communicated by this theological understanding. Stott's response to those who cannot stomach the notion of propitiation is to read carefully the many portions of Scripture that advance the idea (e.g., Rom. 3:24-25; 1 John 2:1-12; 4:10). This close attention allows him to emphasize that

---

1. John R. W. Stott, *The Cross of Christ* (Downers Grove, IL: InterVarsity, 1986).
2. Stott, *The Cross of Christ*, 168ff.

propitiation is regularly described in Scripture as God's work (rather than a work of sinners seeking to turn aside cosmic displeasure). This reading points to God's surpassing consideration for humanity as the key point. In Stott's words, "it cannot be emphasized too strongly that God's love is the source, not the consequence, of the atonement." With this perspective the doctrine assumes a different shape: "So then, God himself is at the heart of our answer to all three questions about the divine propitiation. It is God himself who in holy wrath needs to be propitiated, God himself who in holy love undertook to do the propitiating, and God himself who in the person of his Son died for the propitiation of our sins."[3] In other words, propitiation, rightly understood, reveals God at the center of the drama of redemption, acting both to save sinners and to glorify himself.

For Stott, the four biblical metaphors for salvation combine naturally into a more comprehensive picture of *substitution:* "Moved by the perfection of his holy love, God in Christ substituted himself for us as sinners. That is the heart of the cross of Christ."[4] Again, scriptural phrases are required to express the mystery at the heart of the substitutionary atonement: "On the one hand, God was in Christ reconciling. On the other, God made Christ to be sin for us [cf. 2 Cor. 5:21]. How God can have been in Christ when he made him to be sin is the ultimate mystery of the atonement. But we must hold both affirmations tenaciously, and never expound either in such a way as to contradict the other."[5]

In the cross, Christ triumphed and continues to triumph over the law that reveals human guilt, the flesh that in biblical terms defines spiritual as well as physical weakness, the world that distracts from God, death that threatens life itself, and the devil who exists only to destroy humanity. Divergent conceptions of how the triumph of the cross takes place have led to various theories of the atonement. The moral influence view holds that Christ triumphs over sin by providing the perfect example of self-giving love. Taken by itself as a compre-

---

3. Stott, *The Cross of Christ,* 174, 175.
4. Stott, *The Cross of Christ,* 167.
5. Stott, *The Cross of Christ,* 201.

hensive explanation, however, the moral influence view falls short since this depiction cannot stand up to the challenge succinctly articulated by Anselm: "you have not yet considered the seriousness of sin."[6] The "Christus victor" picture of the atonement, which was memorably expounded in a noteworthy book by the Swedish theologian Gustaf Aulén, holds that the central meaning of atonement is Christ's *victory over sin*.[7] But again, taken by itself, this view is not adequate. In Stott's phrase, "all three of the major explanations of the death of Christ [moral influence, Christ as victor, and substitution] contain biblical truth and can to some extent be harmonized, especially if we observe that the chief difference between them is that in each God's work in Christ is directed towards a different person. In the 'objective' view God satisfies himself, in the 'subjective' he inspires us, and in the 'classic' he overcomes the devil."[8] Yet Stott follows the main insights of the Reformation and many of the main evangelical movements of recent centuries in contending that substitution (or the "objective" view) must be regarded as the key biblical metaphor for the atonement.

Assuming that Stott has correctly described the truly existing situation between God and humans, what difference might it make for Christian scholars in their scholarship? In pondering this question, it seems evident that a substitutionary view of the atonement means more for the humanities, the arts, and the human sciences than for the natural sciences. In general, the natural sciences deal more directly with the realm of creation (what God has made and uninterruptedly sustains) and how that created realm functions. By contrast, the human arenas, in which sin and the need for redemption are more obvious, define intellectual domains where atonement theology makes a greater difference. To be sure, the Scriptures do speak of the creation as also longing to share in divine redemption. It is also true that scientists as persons participate fully in the drama of salvation. But the objects of scientific study in nature are not as directly caught

6. Stott, *The Cross of Christ*, 220.

7. Gustaf Aulén, *Christus Victor: An Historical Study of the Three Main Types of the Idea of Atonement*, trans. A. G. Herbert (New York: Macmillan, 1969; original 1931).

8. Stott, *The Cross of Christ*, 230.

up in that drama as are the objects of study in social scientific, humanistic, and artistic scholarship.

The move from atonement theology to learning more generally can be clarified by summarizing the central elements of "the achievement of the cross."[9]

- First is the fact of substitution. Jesus Christ stands in for humanity as paschal victim; Jesus Christ as the glorified Son of God takes humanity with him into the presence of God.
- Second is the magnitude and deathly seriousness of human sinfulness. Atonement presupposes a sinful breach between God and humanity. Reasoning that ignores this breach must be fatally flawed. At the same time, however, Christian seriousness about the sinful human condition involves surprisingly positive implications about the dignity of humanity. Atonement theology takes sin very seriously indeed, but it also offers a powerful affirmation of human worth. Because in the doctrine of atonement humans are objects of divine love, because God works to overcome sin in order to restore fellowship with himself, we also realize that a theology of the atonement makes a powerful statement about human dignity.
- The third element in atonement theology is the divine initiative in salvation. What is most important for humanity begins with God's grace.
- A fourth element is a strong narrative movement. In Christian theology, the tragedy of the cross becomes the comedy of salvation, and so the drama of salvation can be narrated as either comedy or tragedy. But it must be narrated. Christian salvation is not primarily a matter of categories arranged in order.[10] It is

---

9. Stott, *The Cross of Christ,* 165ff.

10. In this sense, yet another view of the atonement, the "governmental," can be seen as finding genuine insight from biblical accounts that stress the moral equilibrium restored by Christ's sacrifice between divine justice and divine mercy. But this view, which was held by the great seventeenth-century jurist Hugo Grotius and by some of the followers of Jonathan Edwards in the eighteenth and nineteenth centuries, can also be faulted for remaining bloodless in every sense of the term.

rather a matter of actions taken over time. Whether as comedy or tragedy, a religion of the cross affirms a strong sense of purposeful action moving teleologically toward a goal.

• A fifth element in atonement theology is a strong awareness of complexity and multiplicity. Here it is useful to quote Stott, who has well captured both of these realities: "It is essential to keep these two complementary ways of looking at the cross. On the human level, Judas gave him up to the priests, who gave him up to Pilate, who gave him up to the soldiers, who crucified him. But on the divine level, the Father gave him up, and he gave himself up, to die for us."[11] Again, "The Bible includes a number of other phrases which in different ways express this 'duality' within God. He is 'the compassionate and gracious God. . . . Yet he does not leave the guilty unpunished'; in him 'love and faithfulness meet together; righteousness and peace kiss each other.' . . . For 'God is not simply Love. The nature of God cannot be exhaustively stated in one single word' (Brunner)."[12] And again, "The cross was an act simultaneously of punishment and amnesty, severity and grace, justice and mercy."[13] And yet again, "Who am I? . . . I am both noble and ignoble, beautiful and ugly, good and bad, upright and twisted, image and child of God, and yet sometimes yielding obsequious homage to the devil from whose clutches Christ has rescued me. My true self is what I am by creation, which Christ came to redeem, and by calling. My false self is what I am by the Fall, which Christ came to destroy."[14]

If, then, the fact of substitution is a primordial human reality, the seriousness of sin is the essential human dilemma, the divine initiative in salvation is the basis for human hope, the narrative movement of grace is the primary shape for human knowledge, and the complex nature of reality is the inescapable challenge for human un-

11. Stott, *The Cross of Christ,* 61.
12. Stott, *The Cross of Christ,* 130.
13. Stott, *The Cross of Christ,* 159.
14. Stott, *The Cross of Christ,* 285.

derstanding — then the human study of the world should reflect these realities. How might they do so? Here are six possibilities.

1. For social science, theories must be incomplete if they view the solution to human problems as arising *only* from a manipulation of environment. The solution to genuine human problems must involve attention to the moral state of humanity as well as to human circumstances. Since humans are moral creatures defined in substantial part by the coloration of sin, the best social science will always consider intrinsic moral nature as well as extrinsic material influence. Visions of humanity that begin with human innocence — whether from Rousseau, or from Marx, or from rational choice capitalism — will never be adequate as a faithful account of social reality.

2. Whether in the social sciences or the humanities, synchronic (or point in time) analysis will explain a great deal, but such analysis will not explain the full human situation until it is put to use for the sake of diachronic narration (or the movement of events through time). If at the heart of the whole human story is the drama of redemption, then scholarship about humanity must in some form reflect the narrative of God's saving work in Christ.

3. But if atonement theology suggests that narrative is basic to human expression, including artistic expression, the question of narrative shape is also important. Since atonement involves tremendous complexity and great mystery, the best narratives will not be simplistic (like movies where resolution comes through a car chase or gunfight). Neither will the best narratives be Manichean (where the good guys are all good and the bad guys are all bad). Nor will they be simply heroic (where protagonists triumph over obstacles through reliance on their own inner resources) or simply nihilistic (where the point is to enact the futility of human existence as in novels of Thomas Hardy like *Jude the Obscure* and *Tess of the D'Urbervilles*). Rather, the best narratives will be morally complex, as in fact the enduring tragedies, comedies, and novels — like *Oedipus Rex, King Lear, Paradise Lost,* and *Crime and Punishment* — regularly are. Such morally complex narratives are most satisfying because, in terms of atonement theology, they are most true to life.

4. Atonement theology also speaks to the relationship of individ-

uals to community. At least in Western cultures, a certain stress on the individual is needed for human institutions to function well (*my* sin put Christ on the cross; for *me* he died). But theories of home, economics, society, or the state that defer completely to the individual must be inadequate. Principles of individualism are necessary to check the excesses of groups — whether national, ethnic, tribal, ideological, or racial. Humans can be desperately sinful in groups as well as by themselves. But in light of atonement theology, it is ultimately correct for individuals to see themselves as constituent members of groups and for individuals to stand for, stand in for, and represent others. "Corporate" entities, in this broad sense of the term, really do deserve to be treated as "individuals," and in many cases as more important than individuals.

In the Scriptures and in the great Christian traditions, theologies of salvation always stand closely connected to theologies of the church. At this point the ambiguity of the English language is ideal: in English-language Bibles we read that "Christ died for you," where "you" can be taken as either singular or plural. This verbal ambiguity is ideal for expressing the basic reality of human community in the drama of salvation. The same is communicated even more directly throughout the Scriptures. Thus, Christ died for individuals (Rom. 14:15), but also for "all" (2 Cor. 5:15) and for the "we" or "us" who constitute the church (Rom. 5:8). Scholarship faithful to Christian realities will be primed to recognize the communal character of human reality at its most basic level.

5. To expand on earlier comments, for the physical sciences it would seem that theological realities about creation are more directly relevant to scholarship than theological realities about the atonement. Study of the physical world does not involve the moral consequences of sin in the same way that study of humanity does. Therefore, it is difficult to see how the narrative drive of atonement theology says anything specific about the place of development in physical nature. In general, the physical sciences study what *happens* in nature. Most other forms of learning study directly what *happened* in the human community or how contemporary life has been shaped by what *happened* in the past.

6. Finally, since humanity is not morally self-sufficient, theories, narratives, artistic creations, and scholarship that stress the presence of grace as a major element in human existence will be truer to reality than forms that do not. Here we may define "grace" to mean that individuals and groups often receive for their good what they do not deserve to receive. In secular terms we may speak of "fortune" or "luck," but Christian scholars holding to the reality of grace are in better position to understand the true sources of human flourishing.

*   *   *

Whether these six implications hold, or whether I have construed the nature of the atonement adequately, the main point of this exercise is to suggest how doctrine may frame scholarship. The belief that reconciliation with God and, consequently, with fellow humans depends on the death and resurrection of Christ, must of necessity have much to do with how the redeemed scholar approaches the tasks of learning.

FIVE

Christology: A Key to Understanding History

—◦◦◦—

We believe in one God the Father all-powerful, Maker of heaven and of earth, and of all things both seen and unseen. And in one Lord Jesus Christ, the only-begotten Son of God, begotten from the Father before all the ages, light from light, true God from true God, begotten not made, consubstantial with the Father, through whom all things came to be; for us humans and for our salvation he came down from the heavens and became incarnate from the Holy Spirit and the Virgin Mary, became human and was crucified on our behalf under Pontius Pilate; he suffered and was buried and rose up on the third day in accordance with the Scriptures; and he went up into the heavens and is seated at the Father's right hand; he is coming again with glory to judge the living and the dead; his kingdom will have no end.

For all Christian believers, the stake in history is immense. Every aspect of lived Christianity (worship, sacraments, daily godliness, private devotion, religiously inspired benevolence, preaching) and every major theme of Christian theology (the nature of God in relation to the world, the meaning of Christ, the character of salvation, the fate of the universe) directly or indirectly asks how the present relates to the past. As stated often in the Scriptures, what went before is now of the essence for Christian life and practice. So, for example, in 1 Corinthians 10, Paul recounts the story of "our forefathers" who "were all under the cloud and . . . passed through the sea" (v. 1) and yet turned away from God. That narrative, he says, "happened to them as examples and [was] written down as warnings for us" (v. 11). Even more sweeping, though more succinct, are the words from Romans 15:4 — "For everything that was written in the past was written to teach us, so that through endurance and the encouragement of the Scriptures we might have hope."

The critical significance of history for Christianity arises, however, not just from how the past bears upon the present, but even more comprehensively from the historical character of Christianity itself. Before precepts, before doctrines, before ethics, before community — though all these and more have their necessary place — before all else that goes into the makeup of Christianity, there were the acts of God. So it is with existence itself: "In the beginning God created the heavens and the earth" (Gen. 1:1). The prelude to the giving of the law was a demonstration of God's active power: "I am the LORD your God, who brought you out of Egypt, out of the land of slavery. You shall have no other gods before me" (Exod. 20:2-3). The Gospel record of Jesus was, according to the Gospel writer Luke, "handed down to us by those who from the first were eyewitnesses and servants of the word" (Luke 1:2). According to the author of First John, the life proclaimed in Jesus Christ was what "we have seen and heard" (1 John 1:3). According to the Second Epistle of Peter, "We did not follow cleverly invented stories when we told you about the power and coming of our Lord Jesus Christ, but we were eyewitnesses of his majesty" (2 Pet. 1:16). As Paul put it most economically when he was being questioned by Agrippa and Festus about what he claimed was "the sober truth" about Jesus Christ: "it was not done in a corner" (Acts 26:25-26). By inference, then, Christian interest in history writing is a natural consequence of the fact that Christianity is so obviously a religion of historical event.

The creeds summarize this historical material with lapidary succinctness. To suggest how creedal affirmations about the nature of the incarnation and the gracious outworking of redemption offer a place to stand from which to view the tasks of history, this chapter takes up only two of many possibilities: first, the nature of historical knowledge, and second, intra-Christian debates over the doctrine of providence applied to historical writing. In both cases, though the matters at issue can be as contentious as they are complex, the orthodox Christology of the creeds marks out the path to productive historical practice.[1]

Modern Debates about Historical Knowledge

When observing contests between modernists and postmodernists about the nature of historical knowledge, Christian believers may be confident that scriptural religion as summarized in the great creeds defines its own moral and epistemological standards. Traditional Christian faith, in short, does not align easily with the contending positions taken for granted in contemporary intellectual disputes. Unlike postmodernism — exemplified at its extreme by radical forms of multiculturalism — biblical religion holds forthrightly to an ideal of universal truth. Yet unlike modernism — exemplified at its extreme by the overweening objectivism of Enlightenment rationality — biblical religion describes truth as a function of subjective personal relationships.

By holding to traditional Christianity, historians can steer between the Scylla of relativistic postmodernism and the Charybdis of naive Enlightenment positivism. Regarding the former, it is obvious

---

1. In this chapter I have drawn on some material first published as "History," in *Dictionary for Theological Interpretation of the Bible,* ed. Kevin J. Vanhoozer et al. (Grand Rapids: Baker, 2005), 295-99; "Teaching History as a Christian," in *Religion, Scholarship, and Higher Education: Perspectives, Models, and Future Prospects,* ed. Andrea Sterk (Notre Dame, IN: University of Notre Dame Press, 2002), 161-71; and "History Wars I, II, III, IV," *Books & Culture,* May/June 1999, 30-34; July/August 1999, 22-25; September/October 1999, 38-41; November/December 1999, 42-44.

that the extreme application of radically deconstructive views about history would destroy the Christian faith, so postmodernism may be rejected without a qualm. Morality in classic Christian terms rests on a real, God-given natural law, on divine commands like those revealed in the Ten Commandments, or on both. Even more importantly, the heart of the gospel is bound up with a realistic view of history: "if Christ has not been raised, our preaching is useless and so is your faith" (1 Cor. 15:14). Christianity has always displayed an innate tendency toward historical realism, in large part because it depends upon events that believers — in their creeds, their liturgies, their dogmatics, their preaching, their prayers — assert really happened. Moreover, Christian practice is predicated on the tacit assumption that these past events can be known reliably today and can provide meaning for present life (however far distant they occurred in the past).

Yet viewed from the other side, Scripture and the great Christian traditions do not offer unambiguous support for the opponents of postmodernism. Individual biblical passages and the creedal summaries of Christian doctrine unite to affirm serious reservations about modernistic objectivity:

- History is written by people, and people always view the past from the particular vantage point where they stand.
- There are no simple historical facts that are also interesting. Asserting that "there once lived in Judea a rabbi called Jesus" comes close to a simple historical fact, but it is far less interesting and far less complex than the assertion that "Jesus was the Christ of God."
- Although historical knowledge is possible, it is never exhaustive, irreformable, or absolute. The apostle was not speaking directly about questions of historical knowledge in 1 Corinthians 13, but he very well could have been: "For we know in part. . . . Now we see but a poor reflection in a mirror. . . . Now I know in part."

If such limits to historical knowledge are in fact implied by the framework of classical Christianity, then there can never be a simple equation between Christian, biblical understandings of true historical knowledge and Enlightenment notions of hard-edged, objective, fully verified historical knowledge.

In a recent survey of the Western historical canon, Donald Kelley's succinct summary shows why the basic biblical preoccupations create their own standards: "The term, and perhaps the concept, *history* in a Herodotean sense is not used in the Bible, and *philosophy* only once, pejoratively at that, but . . . the term *truth* appears over a hundred times in both the Old and the New Testament . . . and *wisdom* . . . over two hundred times." Kelley continues with an analysis pertinent for the present academic situation, where some forms of Enlightenment rationality have descended from the classical traditions that Kelley contrasts with Christian perspectives. "Classical tradition . . . conceived of truth as conformity to fact and proper meaning, which occasionally corresponds to biblical usage. . . . But most often *truth* [in the Bible] is the word and law of God, which must be obeyed on the grounds of authority. So it was also in the New Testament, especially in the preachings of Paul, where the truth resides in Christ and, in contrast to human 'fables,' 'traditions,' and 'philosophy,' would set men free."[2]

Kelley goes on to note, however, that once Christianity had fully absorbed classical learning, Christian authors also adopted classical understandings of historical truth as the unambiguous conformity of historical statements to factual situations. In the Western world during recent centuries that have been dominated by ideals of scientific Enlightenment, Christian believers have also often committed themselves to notions of history as simple fact. For Protestant evangelicals, this commitment has sometimes taken the form of using historical verification of Christ's resurrection as the linchpin for general apologetics. It has also been common to act as if the trustworthiness of Scripture depended preeminently on results from archeology, language studies, and other research deployed to fend off modern higher criticism. In these instances, confidence in scriptural Christianity rests on procedures and intellectual assumptions strongly influenced by Enlightenment modernity.

2. Donald R. Kelley, *Faces of History: Historical Inquiry from Herodotus to Herder* (New Haven: Yale University Press, 1998), 81.

From the side of postmodernity, however, a different group of contemporary believers has recently explored whether the rejection of Enlightenment objectivity might provide an opening for specifically Christian concerns. This rejection has been carried furthest by John Milbank and others in the school of "radical orthodoxy" who see assumptions of Enlightenment objectivity leading necessarily to anti-Christian forms of violent coercion.[3]

In assessing contemporary debates about historical knowledge, Christian efforts to maneuver through turmoil will remain closer to biblical norms if two overarching realities are kept in view. First, in Scripture God is pictured both as personal and as the source of all truth. Thus, the controversy in much contemporary debate over whether truth should be considered as either objective or subjective represents a false dichotomy. Second, in a scriptural view, because God truly exists, because all human groups exist as creatures made in God's image, and yet because God's existence is always more than the sum of the people he has created, the fact that truth is personal allows for the possibility that it might also be universal. As such, the recognition that all truth claims are indeed perspectival (that they all reflect the viewpoint of dominant or subordinate communities, central or marginalized groups) can be granted along with the belief that some degree of reliable knowledge is possible from the narratives shaped by particular perspectives.

More specifically, classical Christianity can afford an attitude of intellectual *lèse majesté* toward recent debates about historical knowledge. On the one side, believers in biblical religion can affirm that, of course, the Enlightenment rationalists are correct. Humans may certainly come to learn true things, and to make valid moral judgments about events or circumstances in the past. The reasons for this confidence, however, rest not on notions of human competence but on an understanding of divine action. God is the source of all things. Through Christ "all things were made; without him nothing was made that has been made" (John 1:3). Not only does the creative activ-

---

3. See, as prime example, John Milbank, *Theology and Social Theory: Beyond Secular Reason* (Oxford: Blackwell, 1990).

ity of the Son of God stand behind the production of all records useful for history, but in that same Son of God "all things hold together" (Col. 1:17). Because all things do in fact hold together in Jesus Christ, historians who write from one particular time and place about an earlier time and place may actually be connected sufficiently with that past time and place to discover at least partial truth about it.

Moreover, believers worried about the fragility of historical knowledge can take heart from the assurance that the wherewithal for human cultural activity — art, politics, business, history, and much more — was created by God. In the words of First Timothy (4:4-5): "For everything God created is good, and nothing is to be rejected if it is received with thanksgiving, because it is consecrated by the word of God and prayer." To summarize the Enlightenment-sounding implications of such scriptural passages: if the Bible affirms that the creation is good, it is reasonable to assume that we may know that it is good, and, even more basically, that we may know it.

Biblical revelation also contains many statements about the epistemic capacities of humanity that lead to a similar confidence in the possibility of historical knowledge. God created humans with the moral and intellectual capacity to "rule" over the physical creation (Gen. 1:26). God is also the source of human diversity, since from one ancestor he "made every nation . . . that they should inhabit the whole earth; and he determined the times set for them and the exact places where they should live" (Acts 17:26). But that human diversity, as the entire narrative of Scripture underscores, does not prevent people everywhere from learning about God's ongoing historical action aimed at the redemption of his people.

From one angle, therefore, an Enlightenment-friendly conclusion seems like a Christian conclusion. When considering what believers affirm about the nature of the created universe and the epistemological abilities of human beings, Christian faith would seem to fully embrace a religious version of Enlightenment confidence in the perspicacity, the security, and the objectivity of historical knowledge.

Put positively, increased confidence in the truthfulness of historic Christianity — in the religion defined by the Apostles' Creed, the

Nicene Creed, and the Chalcedonian Definition concerning the person of Christ — can set minds at ease about the human ability to understand something about the past. Historical study is not a game. The creeds affirm that God created the world, including the universe of human interactions; that God testified to the noetic capacities of humanity by becoming incarnate in human flesh; and that, by providing for human salvation through the person of Jesus Christ, God showed that people could discover at least partial truth about events and circumstances in the past as well as the present. These creedal realities should inspire confidence that, because of how God has configured the world, research into the past may actually uncover the truth about the past.

Or at least some of the truth some of the time in some circumstances. For, as it happens, the same creedal Christianity that banishes historical skepticism also administers a powerful check to blithe overconfidence about the reach of historical knowledge. The same creeds that justify confidence in the human ability to discover truth through historical research also testify eloquently to human finitude, human fallenness, and human situatedness in particular cultures. For their part, each of these fundamental Christian implications moves in a postmodern direction by agreeing that history writing reflects local circumstances, can never be absolute or complete, and — most of all — can never offer any human the sort of factual or moral knowledge that God alone enjoys.

Simply stated, if Scripture offers in many places full confidence in the human ability to know the past, it is also a quarry for postmodernist assertions undercutting blithe confidence in historical objectivity. Thus, humans are sinners and so empirical recidivists who are "ever hearing, but never understanding . . . ever seeing, but never perceiving" (Isa. 6:9). Freely-chosen moral corruption "darkens" understanding (Eph. 4:18); human sinfulness turns the God-given capacity for knowledge into "blindness" (Isa. 43:8; Matt. 15:14; 2 Pet. 1:9; and many more passages). According to these biblical strands — and they are not insubstantial — humans persistently abandon their capacity for finding the truth in favor of abuses that spring from idolatrous self-interest. Believers, too, are not exempt from the historiographical implications of such passages. Salvation, in orthodox Christian terms, is a gift, not a possession. Thus, although Christians are redeemed, they still suffer from the effects of sinful nature, one of which is the distorting effect of sin on even the believer's ability to view the past objectively and truly.

Another and more positive strand of biblical revelation also seems to reinforce something like a postmodern conclusion about the essentially partial character of historical knowledge. It is the biblical message of the incarnation of the Son of God at a particular time and place and into the particular circumstances of a particular culture. The very particularity of the incarnation inspires the notion that the vast panoply of human cultural differences — the very differences that so often seem incompatible and, thus, the ground for skeptical theories emphasizing multiculturalism — is a gift of God. So it was on the Day of Pentecost when the multiplicity of tongues became an expression of God's many-sided grace, as "each one heard [the disciples] speaking in his own language" (Acts 2:6). Later in the book of Acts, the apostle Peter made a further declaration about the inherent possibility for insight about God found throughout the globe: "I now realize how true it is that God does not show favoritism but accepts men from every nation who fear him and do what is right" (10:34-35). In such passages we seem to hear Scripture saying that cultural diversity, the great stimulator for postmodern conclusions about incompatible readings of history, is from God. The implication for history would seem to be that if different cultures come up with different historiographical conventions, different historical emphases, or different procedures for uniting the present to the past, it is really not a problem.

So, one might ask, does creedal Christianity produce only confusion about the possibility of historical knowledge? Does it merely take away with one hand what it offers with the other? Not at all, for if the heart of Christianity is the incarnation of God the Son, so the heart of historical knowledge is its duality between universal certainties and culturally specific particularities. The incarnation of Jesus Christ *was* a very particular event, circumscribed everywhere by the particular cultural circumstances of its day, and yet believers have always held that this very particular event contains the most grandly universal meaning. This is the conjunction that the missiologists we have already cited emphasize as the key to the worldwide spread of Christian faith.[4] Believers, in other words, should not be surprised if historical work offers the most intimate combination of solidly grounded knowledge with completely contextualized construction.

The challenge to self-awareness in contemporary debates about historical knowledge illustrates the depths of classical Christian dogma. On the one hand, that dogma provides reasons for considerable confidence in the possibility of historical knowledge. On the other, specifically post-Christian thinking helps show how often believers have attempted to exert political or ideological hegemony in ways that contradict the message of the cross standing at the heart of creedal Christianity and so promote self-serving distortions of historical knowledge.

Yet the point in *beginning* with an effort to view problems of historical knowledge *first* from the angle of classical Christology is not merely to inquire how Christian resources may be exploited for use by armies on the field of contemporary intellectual combat. The point is rather to achieve a "Peace of God" that does not take the academy's current state of discussion as the best way of framing the question.

A "Peace of God" for history would seem to require a self-consciously Christian form of chastened realism, with the chastening every bit as serious as the commitment to realism. Such a modest realism should be ready to acknowledge that postmodernist critics have accurately described many forms of self-serving distortions or limitations of historical knowledge. At the same time, it can treat the overreaching hubris of Enlightenment rationality as a heresy rather than the original sin. This Christian stance does not, of course, solve actual controversies of historical fact, specific problems of historical interpretation, or contested applications of historical knowledge. What it does provide is some reassurance about the potential for grasping actual historical fact, however hedged around by self-limiting qualifications. It offers hope for potential progress in moral evaluation of the past, but only if

4. See above, 57.

evaluators are much more attentive to the interpretations of others and much more humble about their own historical certainties than evaluators usually are. This line of reasoning rests, finally, on the awareness, however obscured by idolatrous self-assertion, simple fallibility, and the situatedness of all human existence, that the reason we may come to know something about the past is that the past, like the present, is governed by an all-powerful, all-loving God.

Providence and History Writing

But precisely a biblically inspired confidence in the love of God, which, as the creeds emphasize, inspired the incarnation of the Son and the work of salvation through the Holy Spirit, leads to another set of issues. These issues arise from the believers' confidence that the story of redemption rests on real history and that believers may know that history assuredly. These justified convictions, however, have regularly led to the unjustified belief that it is possible to know and communicate the human past in the same way that the divinely inspired authors of Scripture knew and communicated the past. Misuse of the Christian doctrine of providence is responsible for much of this difficulty.

To be sure, the doctrine of providence is an indispensable dogma of orthodox Christianity. It is of the essence of Christian faith to affirm that God superintends everything that happens in the world. When providence is linked to God's love for the world in general, and for his people in particular, the doctrine also becomes one of the most comforting of all Christian truths. So it is explained in the Heidelberg Catechism:

Q. 27. What do you understand by the providence of God?
The almighty and ever-present power of God whereby he still upholds, as it were by his own hand, heaven and earth together with all creatures, and rules in such a way that leaves and grass, rain and drought, fruitful and unfruitful years, food and drink, health and sickness, riches and poverty, and everything else, come to us not by chance but by his fatherly hand.

Q. 28. What advantage comes from acknowledging God's creation and providence?

We learn that we are to be patient in adversity, grateful in the midst of blessing, and to trust our faithful God and Father for the future, assured that no creature shall separate us from his love, since all creatures are so completely in his hand that without his will they cannot even move.[5]

Yet despite the centrality of this doctrine, problems abound when believers put providence in play for history writing. Most obvious is the problem caused when believers rely, not just on the fact of God's universal rule, but on their own ability to understand the detailed means by which God rules the world. Yet from Eusebius in the early fourth century to Hal Lindsey in the late twentieth century, this problem keeps coming back. Eusebius thought he knew exactly why God had led the emperor Constantine to favor the church. Hal Lindsey thought he knew exactly the scenario through which God would bring history to an end. But they were wrong. The general lesson is that when humans assume that their interpretations of history possess the same level of veracity about God and his purposes as the veracity found in Scripture, there are always real difficulties.

The cause of these difficulties can be explained by orthodox theology. It is a basic Christian doctrine that the history inspired by God in Scripture is unique. The Bible discloses the divine purpose for human events in a way that no ordinary history can do. Likewise, it is a basic Christian belief that all humans, including believers, lack the wisdom, foresight, and hindsight that God through the Holy Spirit bestowed on the writers of Scripture. The prophet Isaiah summarized the matter with finality:

"For my thoughts are not your thoughts,
　　neither are your ways my ways," declares the LORD.
"As the heavens are higher than the earth,

5. *The Heidelberg Catechism,* trans. Allen O. Miller and M. Eugene Osterhaven (Philadelphia: United Church, 1962), as reprinted in *Confessions and Catechisms of the Reformation,* ed. Mark A. Noll (Grand Rapids: Baker, 1991), 141-42.

so are my ways higher than your ways
and my thoughts than your thoughts."

(55:8-9)

When humans try to write history as if they were inspired by the Holy Spirit, the result is foolishness (e.g., countless false sightings of the Antichrist), disastrous violence (e.g., arising from the conviction that God is fighting for our side), or a contradiction of the gospel (e.g., the history of only my denomination or faction or country has been guided by God).

A second difficulty in bringing a Christian doctrine of providence to bear on the tasks of history arises from the persistent threat of Manicheism, or the fallacy that the world can be divided simply into a portion governed by God and another portion not governed by God. Against such heresy, the Christian doctrine of providence affirms that God governs all — the actions of those who know and worship him as well as the actions of those who have never heard of him, the actions directly related to the history of salvation and the actions not so related, the actions of believers and the actions of unbelievers. Instead, the proper biblical distinction is between God's common grace, which reveals much about the world to all people, and God's work of redemption, which he makes known through special revelation. To avoid the Manichean impulse, Christian historians need to embrace the fullness of divine providence — as governing alike the development of agriculture in tenth-century pre-Christian China and the amazing expansion of Christianity in contemporary post-Mao China.

A third problem in putting providence to use for history writing involves the relationship of theological conviction to historical analysis, since there are better and worse ways of putting theology to use as a guide for history. The worse ways are intuitive, not spelled out, and reflexive. They produce situations where definite theological convictions overwhelm the contingencies of research and foreordain the character of interpretation.

The better ways of using theological convictions in historical analysis are deductive, spelled out, and self-conscious. They produce situations where writers publicly state the theological convictions they bring to bear in analyzing a particular historical event and where self-consciousness exists about how much any particular bit of research evidence can be allowed to adjust the interpretations required by the historian's theological convictions. Unfortunately, there are not as many examples of such self-conscious and self-critical use of theology for historical analysis as of the intuitive and presumptuous use, but some do exist. In the second half of the sixteenth century, for example, the Lutheran John Sleidan and the Huguenot Lancelot du Voisin, sieur de la Popelinière, both wrote self-consciously as Protestants, yet each also thought he could see evidence pointing to some basic similarities between Catholics and Protestants. For expressing such opinions, they were blasted by both Catholics and Protestants.[6]

A final problem in guiding historical work by a Christian doctrine of providence is the confusion that exists when trying to sort out the various ways in which believers may think of providence and bring providence to bear on their historical work. As an effort to clarify this confusion, a four-cell matrix, divided into squares by two axes, can show that there are actually *four different types* of legitimately providential history.

Varieties of Providential History

INTERPRETATION

	Special Revelation	General Revelation
History of Christianity		
General History		

SUBJECT MATTER

---

6. A. G. Dickens and John M. Tonkin, *The Reformation in Historical Thought* (Cambridge: Harvard University Press, 1985), 16, 84.

The first axis differentiates *interpretive questions* between historians oriented primarily to special revelation (which is seen by the eye of faith) and historians oriented primarily to general revelation (which can be seen by all). A concentration on special revelation characterizes historians who carry out their work with theological convictions about the church, salvation, the means of grace, and the course of the gospel uppermost in their minds. They are seeking to describe what God is doing in the world. The contrast is with historians who carry out their work with theological convictions about God's general creation of the world, the structures of human cultures, and the natural tasks of all humans uppermost in their minds. They are using procedures open to all humans, whether Christian or not, even as they regard these procedures as originating in God's creative actions and sustained by his ongoing providence.

Historians orienting their interpretive questions by general revelation do not usually refer as directly to Scripture for warrants justifying their work as do historians working with standards of special revelation, but they could do so. Scriptural accounts spelling out where God ordained the ordinary practices of normal human life are the relevant passages, for example:

> Genesis 2:15-25, where God situates Adam (= "the man") in the spheres of agriculture (and by extension, labor in general), religion, intellectual life (naming the animals), and family life.
>
> Genesis 4:17-22, where many artifacts of human culture, which later in Scripture are used for the service of God, are created by nonbelievers who do not know God; these include the construction of cities, the raising of livestock, the use of music, and the making of metal tools.
>
> Exodus 31:1-11, where two lay workmen, Bezalel and Oholiab, are described as "filled . . . with the Spirit of God, with skill, ability and knowledge in all kinds of crafts" (v. 3) as they demonstrate their skill in metallurgy, jewelry making, chemistry, architecture, and other crafts to build the tabernacle.

Such passages about the ordinary tasks of ordinary human life (and there are many more) reinforce the Christian truth that providence extends to all things, even to interpretive questions oriented toward the domain of general revelation.

The second axis pertinent for a consideration of providence and history writing defines a difference of *subject matter*. The difference is between subjects in the history of Christianity and subjects in general history. Extensive discussion is not required to spell out this difference, for it is obvious — the difference, for example, in researching George Whitefield, known everywhere in the eighteenth century for his exuberant promotion of evangelical Christianity, and in researching the French and Indian or Seven Years' War, the eighteenth-century imperial struggle that, even if it had definite religious aspects, is usually studied for its role in military, economic, imperial, national, or political developments. The essential thing to be said by Christian scholars about this distinction is that both the history of Christianity and more general history — both the career of Whitefield and the unfolding of the Seven Years' War — were governed by God's providential care.

With these axes in place — dividing interpretive questions and dividing subject matter, yet all reflecting the workings of providence — it is possible to define four kinds of providential history that Christian believers have in fact been writing for quite some time. In a diagram the four cells would be labeled as follows:

- History of Christianity oriented toward interpretive questions defined by special revelation (what is seen by the eye of faith)
- General history oriented toward interpretive questions defined by special revelation (what is seen by the eye of faith)
- General history oriented toward interpretive questions defined by general revelation (what can be seen by all)
- History of Christianity oriented toward interpretive questions defined by general revelation (what can be seen by all)

Christian controversies over historical writing have often been acrimonious and unproductive because of a failure to acknowledge that historical efforts by other believers were emphasizing other aspects of providence. For example, a sharp exchange that took place between Iain Murray and Harry Stout over Stout's 1991 biography of

George Whitefield stemmed from a basic difference between Murray's history of Christianity featuring interpretive questions oriented toward special revelation and Stout's history of Christianity featuring interpretive questions oriented toward general revelation.[7]

More fruitful critical analysis comes from recognizing that standards for evaluating histories need to be specific to the particular kind of providential history attempted. While recognizing the difficulty of characterizing the work of individual historians, it may still be possible to specify individual books and historians whose work exemplifies each kind of history.

Perhaps the best history of Christianity oriented toward interpretive questions defined by special revelation now being written comes from the missiologist Andrew Walls.[8] By specifying the overarching Christian doctrines he takes as norms for his historical work — especially the doctrine of the incarnation — and then by carrying out wide-ranging research to illustrate the bearing of the incarnation for historical developments in many times and many places, Walls provides, as it were, a God's-eye view of great swaths of human history and does so with greatly stimulating historical insight.

As a reminder that any such scheme for classification is only heuristic, it may not be as easy to characterize the work of other notable missiological historians like Kenneth Scott Latourette, Lamin Sanneh, and Dana Robert.[9] They can be evaluated almost as highly as Andrew Walls as historians of Christianity oriented toward interpretive questions defined by special revelation, but because their work sometimes places more emphasis on research keyed to analysis open

---

7. Iain H. Murray, "Explaining Evangelical History," *Banner of Truth,* July 1994, 8-14; Harry Stout, letter to the editor, *Banner of Truth,* March 1995, 7-10; Murray, response to Stout, *Banner of Truth,* March 1995, 10-11.

8. Andrew F. Walls, *The Missionary Movement in Christian History* (Maryknoll, NY: Orbis, 1996); *The Cross-Cultural Process in Christian History* (Maryknoll, NY: Orbis, 2002).

9. For example, Kenneth Scott Latourette, *A History of the Expansion of Christianity,* 7 vols. (New York: Harper and Bros., 1937-1945); Lamin O. Sanneh, *Abolitionists Abroad: American Blacks in the Making of West Africa* (Cambridge: Harvard University Press, 1999); Dana L. Robert, *Christian Mission: How Christianity Became a World Religion* (Malden, MA: Wiley-Blackwell, 2009).

to all interpreters, non-Christian as well as Christian, they can also be treated as historians of Christianity whose interpretive questions are normed more by general revelation than by special revelation.

Another variety of exemplary missiological history oriented toward interpretive questions defined by special revelation comes from modern accounts of the spread of Christianity in the Two-Thirds World. Provocative writing by the late Ogbu Kalu challenged the ordinary procedures of Western historiography with an appeal to recognize that much of the dynamic history of Christianity is now being enacted in cultures where Enlightenment notions of the possible never took root.[10] Kalu suggests that a history of Christianity that is faithful to the ordinary experiences of believers in the Two-Thirds World must somehow combine the sort of natural analysis well honed in Western historiography with a species of supernatural analysis shaped by the day-to-day realities of Christianity in the developing world.

The kind of disciplined, self-conscious providential history for which Kalu appeals would look a great deal like the history in Richard Lovelace's 1979 book *Dynamics of Spiritual Life*.[11] With its wide-ranging research into the history of evangelicalism and its interpretations keyed to theological convictions about ecclesiastical renewal, Lovelace did for the history of Western evangelicalism what Kalu proposed for the history of emerging world Christianities.

The books of contemporary historians like Iain Murray or earlier historians like John Foxe from the sixteenth century are also exemplary representatives of the history of Christianity guided by interpretive questions oriented toward special revelation.[12] By comparison with the books of the missiologists, however, their work is likely to be less broadly appealing since the theological convictions guiding their

10. For example, Ogbu Kalu, *Clio in a Sacred Garb: Essays on Christian Presence and African Responses, 1900-2000* (Trenton, NJ: Africa World Press, 2008), and *African Pentecostalism: An Introduction* (New York: Oxford University Press, 2008).

11. Richard F. Lovelace, *Dynamics of Spiritual Life: An Evangelical Theology of Renewal* (Downers Grove, IL: InterVarsity, 1979).

12. John Foxe, *The Book of Martyrs* (major editions, 1563, 1570, 1583), and, for example, Iain Murray, *David Martyn Lloyd-Jones*, 2 vols. (Edinburgh: Banner of Truth, 1982, 1990).

efforts are narrower. Not the incarnation, which has been central in all Christian traditions, but in Foxe's case the principles of the English Reformation (and so excluding Roman Catholics) and in Murray's case the principles of the twentieth-century Puritan revival (and so excluding all who do not bring with them to historical interpretation the norms of that kind of Calvinism) are the operative theological convictions.

In general, histories of Christianity oriented toward interpretive questions defined by special revelation are most persuasive for audiences that share the same theological convictions as the authors of these histories. While it is true that all historians bring the equivalent of theological convictions to their work, the more specific those convictions are, the more they turn history into theology teaching by example. It is the same with strongly Marxist, strongly feminist, strongly gay, or strongly nationalistic history. While extensive research may go into the writing of such works, it will be the strongly held ideology that guides the final interpretation.

Historical work falling into the second cell is different. Over the last century there have been a number of exemplary practitioners of general history oriented toward interpretive questions defined by the norms of special revelation. Of course, there have also been many bad examples, especially those historians who with partisan research and short-circuited reasoning enlist God as a promoter of German, Russian, British, or American national history. But it is more edifying to contemplate the good examples, which include, at a minimum:

- Christopher Dawson, who brought the convictions of modern Neo-Thomism to bear in studying the rise and decline of western European civilizations;
- James Juhnke, who brought Anabaptist convictions to bear in studying the wars of America;
- Steven Keillor, who brought the convictions of a moderately dispensational Brethrenism to bear on all of American history;
- Richard John Neuhaus, who brought neoconservative and Catholic convictions to bear on the meaning of America in world history;

- Christopher Shannon, who brought Catholic traditionalist convictions to bear on writing the history of modern American intellectual life; and
- Aleksandr Solzhenitsyn, who brought Russian Orthodox convictions to bear in studying the twentieth-century history of Russia.[13]

These authors have shared a belief that they can indeed see the hand of providence at work, but in general developments of world history. Because that seeing is self-conscious, sophisticated, or qualified by a willingness to engage research and interpretation from those of other points of view, it succeeds as good history as well as often persuasive polemic.

The next cell, general history oriented toward interpretive questions defined by general revelation, is the hardest one to discuss, because its practitioners neither write directly on topics in the history of Christianity nor usually draw attention to their convictions about theological matters as such. Yet even though it is difficult to name examples of this type, it may be the most widely practiced kind of providential history. Arthur Link, the biographer of Woodrow Wilson, was a representative. His work on Wilson and Wilson's papers was oriented toward general American history and the significance of Wilson for American national history, but Link openly carried out his work as a distinct Christian vocation.[14] Daniel Walker Howe, author of several highly regarded works on American politics and intellectual life in the period between the Revolution and the Civil War, might be included

13. For example, Christopher Dawson, *Understanding Europe* (New York: Sheed and Ward, 1952); James C. Juhnke and Carol M. Hunter, *The Missing Peace: The Search for Nonviolent Alternatives in United States History* (Kitchener, Ontario: Pandora, 2001); Steven J. Keillor, *God's Judgments: Interpreting History and the Christian Faith* (Downers Grove, IL: InterVarsity, 2007); Richard John Neuhaus, *The Naked Public Square* (Grand Rapids: Eerdmans, 1984), and subsequent discussion of this book; Christopher Shannon, *Conspicuous Criticism: Tradition, the Individual, and Culture in Modern American Society Thought*, 2nd ed. (Chicago: University of Chicago Press, 2006); Aleksandr Solzhenitsyn, *The Oak and the Calf* (New York: Harper and Row, 1980).

14. For example, Arthur S. Link, *Woodrow Wilson and the Progressive Era, 1910-1917* (New York: Harper, 1954).

as another representative. His subject matter often touches on religion, sometimes significantly, but the burden of his work is to interpret American history to broad audiences rather than specifically Christian audiences. Yet Howe's attachment to Christian faith and his willingness to have Christian norms shape the direction of his work are noticeable features of much that he has written.[15]

The final cell, history of Christianity oriented toward interpretive questions defined by general revelation, is now jammed with exemplary practitioners. The wide-ranging work of historians in this cell is defined by treatment of events, people, or problems in the history of Christianity marked by broadly ranging research and interpretations aimed at general audiences rather than particular faith communities. Specified more particularly, it is history written for audiences where theological or ideological convictions are looser rather than tighter, broad rather than specific, ecumenical rather than sectarian. In theological terms, this kind of history emphasizes more the secondary causes through which God governs the world rather than the immediate narrative of redemption.

In their combination of subject matter and method these historians represent an instantiation of Christian practice within the cultural conventions of modern Western thought. They have accommodated themselves to the focus on nature, on this-worldly causes and effects, and on universal human values that have characterized Western societies since the eighteenth century. Yet they are also easily distinguished from secular historians guided by non-Christian convictions. These historians do feature interpretations drawing on intellectual, economic, cultural, social, and political factors, but do not reduce religious motives and practices to supposedly more real spheres of human existence. They likewise treat their subjects, both Christian and non-Christian, as agents of dignity made in the image of God. While their works are not overtly dogmatic or evangelistic, they are often easily perceived as reflecting a Christian frame of reference, especially by letting their Christian subjects speak for them-

15. For example, Daniel Walker Howe, *What Hath God Wrought: The Transformation of America, 1815-1848* (New York: Oxford University Press, 2007).

selves, by interpreting the factors that shape their subjects as penulti-
mate rather than ultimate realities, and by acknowledging their own
respect for (or even adherence to) Christian beliefs.

This type of history is providential because its practitioners indicate, either explicitly or implicitly, that they are carrying on their historical work with procedures made possible by God and with conclusions describing a world in which God is an ever-present reality.

It is risky to attempt a list of historians who practice this kind of
history, in part because of chagrin about inevitable omissions, in part
because not all historians who might fit this designation would ac-
cept it for themselves. But historians who work on Christian subjects
with the norms of general revelation would seem to include Katherine
Clay Bassard, Margaret Bendroth, Edith Blumhofer, Catherine
Brekus, Joel Carpenter, Richard Carwardine, Eamon Duffy, Philip
Gleason, Brad Gregory, Allen Guelzo, Nathan Hatch, Charles
Hambrick-Stowe, David Hempton, Mark Hutchinson, Robert Linder,
George Marsden, John McGreevy, Jaroslav Pelikan, Richard Pierard,
Stuart Piggin, George Rawlyk, Jeffrey Burton Russell, Timothy Smith,
Dale Van Kley, Grant Wacker, and many more.[16]

---

16. As examples, Katherine Clay Bassard, *Transforming Scriptures: African Ameri-
can Women Writers and the Bible* (Athens: University of Georgia Press, 2010); Margaret
Bendroth, *Fundamentalism and Gender: 1875 to the Present* (New Haven: Yale University
Press, 1993); Edith Blumhofer, *Everybody's Sister: Aimee Semple McPherson* (Grand
Rapids: Eerdmans, 1993); Catherine Brekus, *Strangers and Pilgrims: Female Preaching
in America, 1740-1845* (Chapel Hill: University of North Carolina Press, 1998); Joel A.
Carpenter, *Revive Us Again: The Reawakening of American Fundamentalism* (New York:
Oxford University Press, 1997); Richard Carwardine, *Evangelicals and Politics in Ante-
bellum America* (New Haven: Yale University Press, 1993); Eamon Duffy, *The Stripping of
the Altars: Traditional Religion in England, 1400-1580* (New Haven: Yale University Press,
1992); Philip Gleason, *Contending with Modernity: Catholic Higher Education in the
Twentieth Century* (New York: Oxford University Press, 1995); Brad S. Gregory, *Salvation
at Stake: Christian Martyrdom in Early Modern Europe* (Cambridge: Harvard University
Press, 1999); Allen Guelzo, *Abraham Lincoln: Redeemer President* (Grand Rapids: Eerdmans, 1993); Nathan O. Hatch, *The Democratization of American Christianity* (New Haven: Yale University Press, 1989); Charles Hambrick-Stowe, *The Practice of Piety; Puritan Devotional Disciplines in Seventeenth-Century New England* (Chapel Hill: University
of North Carolina Press, 1982); David Hempton, *Methodism: Empire of the Spirit* (New
Haven: Yale University Press, 2005); Mark Hutchinson, *Iron in Our Blood: A History of the*

Among these historians major differences exist in approach, in interpretation, in selection of significant events to study, and in salience of Christian consciousness. But together they represent a particularly solid phalanx of this kind of providential history.

The character of their providential stance is revealed by the criticism they receive. Some secularists chastise their work as simple dogmatism. Sometimes the criticism is expressed, as from Bruce Kuklick, a friendly critic of self-defined Christian historians, that such work is subpar, or even cowardly, for treating the supernaturalist beliefs of their Christian subjects uncritically.[17] But even stronger criticism comes from historians of Christianity oriented toward interpretive questions defined by special revelation. To such ones the historians who employ categories of general revelation can look like syncretists illegitimately subjecting Christian themes to sub-Christian or even anti-Christian categories. In response, historians of Christianity oriented more toward general revelation can say that they perceive a great deal of mystery in the whole process of redemption, which makes them wary of being too dogmatic about specifying what God is

---

Presbyterian Church in New South Wales, 1788-2001 (Sydney: Ferguson, 2001); Robert Linder, *The Long Tragedy: Australian Evangelical Christians and the Great War, 1914-1918* (Adelaide: Openbook, 2000); George M. Marsden, *Jonathan Edwards: A Life* (New Haven: Yale University Press, 2003); John T. McGreevy, *Catholicism and American Freedom: A History* (New York: Norton, 2003); Jaroslav Pelikan, *Jesus through the Centuries* (New Haven: Yale University Press, 1985); Richard V. Pierard and Robert D. Linder, *Civil Religion and the Presidency* (Grand Rapids: Academie, 1988); Stuart Piggin, *Evangelical Christianity in Australia: Spirit, Word, and World* (New York: Oxford University Press, 1996); George A. Rawlyk, *The Canada Fire: Radical Evangelicalism in British North America, 1775-1812* (Kingston/Montreal: McGill-Queen's University Press, 1994); Jeffrey Burton Russell, *A History of Heaven: The Singing Silence* (Princeton: Princeton University Press, 1997); Timothy L. Smith, *Revivalism and Social Reform: American Protestantism on the Eve of the Civil War* (Baltimore: Johns Hopkins University Press, 1980; original 1957); Dale Van Kley, *The Religious Origins of the French Revolution: From Calvin to the Civil Constitution, 1560-1791* (New Haven: Yale University Press, 1996); Grant Wacker, *Heaven Below: Early Pentecostals and American Culture* (Cambridge: Harvard University Press, 2001).

17. See, for example, Bruce Kuklick, "On Critical History," in *Religious Advocacy and American History,* ed. Kuklick and D. G. Hart (Grand Rapids: Eerdmans, 1997), 54-64.

doing even in the institutions and activities of the church. The response could even go so far as to reverse the charge: that historians of Christianity focused on special revelation have taken Enlightenment norms of comprehensibility and human knowledge into the precincts of divine mystery. Historians of Christianity focused on general revelation, in other words, would likely approve of how the *Catechism of the Catholic Church* describes the relationship between events in the history of salvation, like the resurrection of Christ, and the events of ordinary history: "No one was an eyewitness to Christ's Resurrection and no evangelist describes it. No one can say how it came about physically. Still less was its innermost essence, his passing over to another life, perceptible to the senses. Although the Resurrection was an historical event that could be verified by the sign of the empty tomb and by the reality of the apostles' encounters with the risen Christ, still it remains at the very heart of the mystery of faith as something that transcends and surpasses history."[18]

Much more debate is possible between and among practitioners of these four types of providential history. When, however, attention is directed to the different levels at which providence operates and to its boundless extent, occasions for criticism fade. The remarkable thing in our day is how vigorously each of the four types of providential history is being pursued.

*　　*　　*

These efforts to examine modern debates over historical knowledge from a christological perspective and to parse the meaning of providence for history writing into four types follow a path opened by the creeds. The incarnation joins particularity and universality; the Christian concept of providence encompasses all of creation as well as the narrative of redemption. The path opened by these realities is broad and inviting, although it would contradict the creeds themselves to claim that any one journey along this path is a path that all believers must follow.

---

18. *Catechism of the Catholic Church* (Liguori, MO: Liguori, 1994), 169 (par. 647).

SIX

"Come and See": A Christological Invitation for Science

———ⱷⱷⱷ———

We believe in one God the Father all-powerful, Maker of heaven and of earth, and of all things both seen and unseen. And in one Lord Jesus Christ . . . , through whom all things came to be. . . .

[W]e all with one voice teach the confession of one and the same Son, our Lord Jesus Christ: the same perfect in divinity and perfect in humanity, the same truly God and truly man, of a rational soul and a body; consubstantial with the Father as regards his divinity, and the same consubstantial with us as regards his humanity; like us in all respects except for sin; begotten before the ages from the Father as regards his divinity, and in the last days the same for us and for our salvation from Mary, the Virgin God-bearer as regards his humanity; one and the same Christ, Son, Lord, Only-begotten, acknowledged in two natures which undergo no confusion, no change, no division, no separation; at no point was the difference between the natures taken

away through the union, but rather the property of both natures is preserved and comes together into a single person
and a single subsistent being; he is not parted or divided
into two persons, but is one and the same only-begotten
Son, God, Word, Lord Jesus Christ. . . .

The bearing of Christology on science involves historical as well as
theological awareness. Historical awareness is required because
the relationship between God's "two books," Scripture and nature, has
changed significantly over the course of centuries between biblical
times and the present. So long as Christian communities thought it was
a straightforward task to harmonize what Scripture seemed to communicate about the natural world and what observing nature or reflecting
on nature seemed to communicate, the discussion was contained.

This situation, with some exceptions, largely prevailed until the
sixteenth century and the beginnings of the modern scientific era. Yet
even in the centuries when challenges to a "literal" reading of Scripture were still relatively few, perceptive believers knew that considerable sophistication was necessary to bring together biblical interpretation and interpretations of nature. Thus, early in the fifth century,
Saint Augustine noted that perceptive non-Christians really did know
a great deal about "the earth, the heavens, and the other elements of
the world, about the motion and orbit of the stars and even their size
and relative positions, about the predictable eclipses of the sun and
moon, the cycles of the years and the seasons, about the kinds of animals, shrubs, stones, and so forth." Given such able observers, he
held it was "a disgraceful and dangerous thing for an infidel to hear a
Christian, presumably giving the meaning of Holy Scripture, talking
nonsense on these topics." When this kind of nonsense proliferated,
the great danger was that those outside the faith would believe that
the Scriptures themselves ("our sacred writers") taught the nonsense
and so would be put off from the life-giving message of the Bible. Augustine expressed this danger in this way: "If they find a Christian
mistaken in a field which they themselves know well and hear him
maintaining his foolish opinions about our books, how are they going

to believe those books in matters concerning the resurrection of the dead, the hope of eternal life, and the kingdom of heaven, when they think their pages are full of falsehoods on facts which they themselves have learnt from experience and the light of reason?" His closing injunction was to chastise "reckless and incompetent expounders of Holy Scripture" who "defend their utterly foolish and obviously untrue statements" by calling on "Holy Scripture for proof and even recit[ing] from memory many passages which they think support their position."[1] Yet comparatively speaking, in Augustine's own lifetime and for long thereafter, there were relatively few occasions when efforts at uniting scriptural teaching with knowledge gained from study of nature posed great difficulties.

That situation changed when the results of modern science called into question a growing array of straightforward, or "literal," interpretations of the Bible. From the sixteenth century onward, the number of apparent problems accumulated. Hard-won conclusions in the natural sciences, gained through ever more intense and ever more sophisticated study of nature, seemed to contradict what the Scriptures taught. Thus, the earth was the center of neither the solar system nor the entire universe (as might be concluded from some biblical passages); the earth was billions of years old (not of recent vintage); the universe was unimaginably vast (not sized by human scale); animal "species" designated temporary way stations on continuously changing paths of evolutionary development (not permanently fixed entities); human beings were part of this evolutionary development (not a species distinct in every way from animals).

As these seeming contradictions became urgent in the development of modern science, believers wrestled long and hard to keep what was learned from nature and what was learned from Scripture in sync. While the difficulties for each particular question involving Scripture and nature were important, it is even more important to re-

---

1. *St. Augustine, "The Literal Meaning of Genesis,"* 2 vols., translated and annotated by John Hammond Taylor, S.J. (New York: Newman, 1982), 1:42-43. The quotations from Augustine and Galileo in this chapter are repeated from *The Scandal of the Evangelical Mind* because they are two of the sanest authoritative analyses ever uttered on the "problem" of Christianity and science.

member that they mattered only because of the larger framework spelled out by Saint Augustine. Since Scripture described the new life offered in Christ, which was the most important thing for all humans in all of history, to cast substantial doubt on Scripture for secondary concerns was to shake confidence in what the Bible revealed concerning the most important matter. Yet once that relationship between Scripture on all things (including nature) and Scripture on the most important thing (reconciliation with God in Christ) is kept in view, progress may be possible on issues involving Scripture and science. The key is that if Christ is the central and unifying theme of Scripture, then Christ should be preeminent in understanding scriptural revelation about everything else, including nature.

To view scientific exploration as a christological concern, it is helpful first to explore historical reasons for the difficulties besetting efforts at bringing scientific knowledge and biblical wisdom together. We will briefly explore some of that history as a prelude to the positive presentation, which begins with a case study from the career of the conservative Presbyterian theologian B. B. Warfield. Warfield, who taught at Princeton Theological Seminary in the late nineteenth and early twentieth centuries, is significant for our purposes because of how he deployed a crucial stance developed in thinking about Jesus when he came to evaluate modern theories of evolutionary development. The chapter ends by suggesting how explicit christological perspectives might guide Christian believers in thinking about the workings of science.

The Bible and Science Historically Considered

Of the many books that have treated the record of religious-science engagement since the sixteenth century, the best have demonstrated that there has never been a simple conflict between biblical theology and natural science.[2] Rather, that history has been marked by a sus-

---

2. See especially John Hedly Brooke, *Science and Religion: Some Historical Perspectives* (New York: Cambridge University Press, 1991); David C. Lindberg and Ron-

tained series of negotiations, breakthroughs, well-publicized flash-points, much conceptual rethinking, lots of ignorant grandstanding, some intellectual overreaching by starry-eyed avatars of a supremely all-competent "Science," some intellectual overreaching by determined "defenders" of Scripture, much noncontroversial science carried out by Christians, a huge quantity of scientific advance accepted routinely by believers, and much more.

At the dawn of modern science in the early seventeenth century, the iconic experimenter and polemicist Galileo Galilei recorded exceedingly wise words about how to combine investigations of nature with complete trust in Scripture. Implicit in his comments was an anchorage in christological realities that I hope to make explicit at the end of this chapter. If Galileo's guidelines had been followed, the history of science and religion in the modern West would have been much calmer than what actually unfolded. Galileo's comments are worth quoting in full before exploring why it has been so difficult to follow his proposals for peace between belief in Scripture and reliance on the results of scientific investigation. His standpoint combined a number of basic dispositions:

- trust that sense experience, rigorously controlled and creatively contemplated, could reveal truths about nature;
- trust that biblical interpretation and scientific interpretation cannot in principle conflict because God is the author of both Scripture and nature;
- realization that much in the Bible is not intended as a scientific description of the world;
- realization that interpretation of Scripture and interpretation of nature often require legitimately different procedures; and

---

ald L. Numbers, eds., *God and Nature: Historical Essays on the Encounter between Christianity and Science* (Berkeley: University of California Press, 1986); and David C. Lindberg and Ronald L. Numbers, eds., *When Science and Christianity Meet* (Chicago: University of Chicago Press, 2003). An excellent reference work is Gary B. Ferngren, ed., *The History of Science and Religion in the Western Tradition: An Encyclopedia* (New York: Garland, 2000).

• confidence that what God allows humans to learn about nature could help discern what God has revealed in Scripture.

Here is what Galileo wrote:

It is most pious to say and most prudent to take for granted that Holy Scripture can never lie, as long as its true meaning has been grasped; but I do not think one can deny that this is frequently recondite and very different from what appears to be the literal meaning of the words. . . . I think that in disputes about natural phenomena one must begin not with the authority of scriptural passages but with sensory experience and necessary demonstrations. For the Holy Scripture and nature derive equally from the godhead, the former as the dictation of the Holy Spirit and the latter as the most obedient executrix of God's orders; moreover, to accommodate the understanding of the common people it is appropriate for Scripture to say many things that are different (in appearance and in regard to the literal meaning of the words) from the absolute truth; on the other hand, nature is inexorable and immutable, never violates the terms of the laws imposed upon her, and does not care whether or not her recondite reasons and ways of operating are disclosed to human understanding; but not every scriptural assertion is bound to obligations as severe as every natural phenomenon; finally, God reveals Himself to us no less excellently in the effects of nature than in the sacred words of Scripture . . . ; and so it seems that a natural phenomenon which is placed before our eyes by sensory experience or proved by necessary demonstrations should not be called into question, let alone condemned, on account of scriptural passages whose words appear to have a different meaning.

However, by this I do not wish to imply that one should not have the highest regard for passages of Holy Scripture; indeed, after becoming certain of some physical conclusions, we should use these as very appropriate aids to the correct interpretation of Scripture and to the investigation of the truths they must contain, for they are most true and agree with demonstrated truths. . . . I do not think one has to believe that the same God who has given us senses, language, and intellect would want to set aside the use of these and give us by other means the information we can acquire with them, so that we would deny our senses and reason even in the case of those physical conclusions which are placed before our eyes and intellect by our sensory experiences or by necessary demonstrations.[3]

As helpful as what Galileo said in the early seventeenth century may still be 400 years later, it is obvious that his hopes for smooth sailing on the sea of science-religion interaction have not been realized. The tumults that have arisen, however, are not random or uncaused. Many, in fact, have been propelled by habits of mind established in Western thinking well before the age of scientific revolution or that came to prominence during the era of the Enlightenment. In other words, thinking about science and religion has always been strongly influenced, sometimes absolutely determined, by important assumptions about *how* that thinking should take place.[4]

Because some of these assumptions arose in the Middle Ages, the recondite debates of thirteenth-century Catholic philosophers actually go far in explaining difficulties that continue to this day.[5] One particular dispute that has exerted a great influence on later Western history concerned the relationship of God's being to all other beings. Thomas Aquinas, the Dominican friar who lived from 1225 to 1274, argued that this relationship was *analogical,* that is, while humans and the created world were certainly *like* God in many ways, the essence of God remained ultimately a mystery known only to himself. Aquinas may well have been thinking of the passage in Isaiah 55:9 where the Lord tells the prophet,

3. "Galileo's Letter to the Grand Duchess" (1615), in *The Galileo Affair: A Documentary History,* ed. Maurice A. Finocchiaro (Berkeley: University of California Press, 1989), 92-94.

4. The following paragraphs are taken, with revisions, from Mark A. Noll, "Evangelicals, Creation, and Scripture: An Overview," BioLogos Forum (November 2009), available from biologos.org/uploads/projects/Noll_scholarly_essay.pdf (accessed May 17, 2010).

5. This section relies on Amos Funkenstein, *Theology and the Scientific Imagination from the Middle Ages to the Seventeenth Century* (Princeton: Princeton University Press, 1986), especially 25-31.

As the heavens are higher than the earth,
    so are my ways higher than your ways
    and my thoughts than your thoughts.

The fact that God created the world out of nothing *(creatio ex nihilo)* was a crucial part of Aquinas's argument, because it meant that, while human minds could understand communication from God (i.e., revelation in nature, in Scripture, in Jesus Christ), they could in principle never grasp the essence of God. An interesting by-product of this position, which has taken on surprising relevance in contemporary debates, was Aquinas's understanding of randomness or contingency. Everything in the world, he insisted, happened because of God's direction. But some things happen contingently, or with the appearance of randomness. The logic of their contingency was perfectly clear to God, but because God in his essence is hidden to humans, humans may not be able to grasp how what they perceive as random could be part of God's direction of the universe.

The opposing view was maintained by the Franciscan priest and philosopher Duns Scotus, a younger contemporary of Aquinas who lived from 1266 to 1308. His position argued for the *univocity* of being. The only way to know the essence of anything is through its existence. Although God is much greater and much wiser than humans, his being and the being of all other things share a common essence. God is the creator and redeemer of humans, but his actions toward humans can (at least potentially) be understood reasonably well because the same laws of being apply to God as to everything else; the same way that we explain causation in every other sphere explains how God causes things to act and to be.

Scotus's approach to metaphysics (= the science of being) became, with a few exceptions, the dominant view in later Western history. It was particularly significant when joined to one more principle, this one from the English Franciscan, William of Ockham (1288-1348). Ockham's famous "razor" held that the simplest explanation was always the best explanation ("do not multiply entities unnecessarily"). Applied to science, this principle came to mean that if a natural event is explained adequately by a natural cause, there is no need to think about supernatural causes or even about the transcendent being of God. The combination of these philosophical positions is responsible for an assumption that prevails widely to this day: *once something is explained clearly and completely as a natural occurrence, there is no other realm of being that can allow it to be described in any other way.*

For a very long time, this assumption was not regarded as anti-Christian, since God was considered the creator of nature and the laws of nature as well as the active providential force that kept nature running as he had created it to run. During the Reformation era, Protestants maintained that conviction, but also began to place a new stress on the importance of Scripture for understanding God, themselves, the church, and everything else.[6] That emphasis was one of the important factors accelerating the rise of modern science. In particular, as Protestants set aside symbolic interpretations of Scripture, which had been prominent in the Middle Ages, they stressed straightforward examination of texts in what was often called a literal approach. This approach, in turn, stimulated a similar effort at examining the natural world in such a way that the medieval idea of God communicating to humans through "two books" (nature and Scripture) took on greater force. The assumption that became very important in this process was that *those who believed God created the physical world and revealed himself verbally in Scripture should harmonize in one complete picture what they learned about nature from studying nature and what they learned about nature from studying Scripture.* In both cases, literal knowledge was crucial, along with a belief that sources of literal knowledge could be fitted together harmoniously.

By the late seventeenth century, when science in its early modern form began to expand rapidly, yet a third conviction became important, which was worked out especially in the many efforts that went into constructing *natural theology.*[7] Natural theology was the project of explaining, often in considerable detail, what God's purposes were in creating the various parts of nature. Natural theology became a major

6. See in particular Peter Harrison, *The Bible, Protestantism, and the Rise of Natural Science* (New York: Cambridge University Press, 1998).

7. For particularly astute treatment, see Brooke, *Science and Religion,* 192-225.

enterprise when the earlier assumptions — metaphysical univocity and harmonization of the "two books" — encountered rapidly expanding knowledge about the physical world. Learned believers recognized the potential threat of this expanding knowledge — if scientific investigation could explain how nature worked as a system unto itself, maybe reliance on God and reference to the Scriptures were expendable. In response to this challenge, savants like Cotton Mather in the American colonies (*The Christian Philosopher,* 1721) and William Denham in England (*Physico-Theology,* 1713) offered elaborate explanations for how the structures of the physical and animal worlds revealed God's purposes in creating things as he had made them.

The tradition of natural theology received its most famous exposition in a book by William Paley, an Anglican archdeacon, published in 1802. Its title explained what it was about: *Natural Theology: or, Evidence of the Existence and Attributes of the Deity, collected from the appearances of nature.* Paley's method was to describe features of animal, human, or material life and then to show how these features manifested God's design in and for nature. For example, the fact that animal and human bodies were symmetrical in outward appearance even as their internal organs and functions were asymmetrical provided Paley with "indubitable evidences, not only of design, but of a great deal of attention and accuracy in prosecuting the design."[8] The very important assumption behind the natural theology promoted by Paley was that *not only did God create and providentially order the natural world, but humans could figure out exactly how and why God ordered creation as he did.* This assumption became critically important when later investigators of nature concluded that it was not necessary to think about God's intentions when figuring out how nature worked, and so belief in God was wrongheaded. In turn, those conclusions naturally antagonized the ones who continued to believe in God and therefore insisted either that new discoveries did in fact reveal a providential design or that the new discoveries had to be false.

Perhaps not many today who are engaged with contemporary de-

---

8. William Paley, *Natural Theology,* ed. Matthew D. Eddy and David Knight (New York: Oxford University Press, 2006; original 1802), 101.

bates in science and religion pause to think about historical turning points deep in the past. But the assumptions of univocal metaphysics, harmonization, and natural theology created powerful channels in which much subsequent discussion has flowed.

During recent decades, much of the conflict involving religion and science has resulted from polemicists on all sides carrying deeply entrenched convictions, attitudes, and assumptions into the present. Sorting out ancient mental habits from recent novelties is difficult, however, in part because there are so many different factors feeding into the current situation, and in part because evaluating these factors requires delicately balanced judgments. As examples of broader concerns, the awareness that nonbelievers of several types regularly use the supposedly assured result of modern science to attack traditional Christianity is hardly a baseless fantasy. In addition, Christian believers of all sorts can only applaud the devotion to Scripture that has been so prominent in conservative Protestant history, but many believers today — including a growing number of evangelicals — question some of the assumptions about how best to interpret Scripture that evangelicals sometimes treat as interchangeable with trust in Scripture itself.

When considered historically, however, it seems obvious that the modern strength of young-earth Creation Science is almost entirely explainable as the continuation of former predispositions.[9] To be sure, skillful publications like John Whitcomb and Henry Morris's *The Genesis Flood,* which appeared in 1961, have added new elements to the mix. And of course, they have been matched blow for blow by skillful antitheistic works like Richard Dawkins's *The God Delusion* that was published in 2006.

Yet the terms of debate in this modern polemical literature depend almost entirely on assumptions about metaphysical univocity, harmonization, and natural theology — as applied to modern questions and disseminated by democratic appeals to a broader public. In

---

9. For the best history, see Ronald L. Numbers, *The Creationists,* expanded ed. (Cambridge: Harvard University Press, 2006), and for a solid general survey, Michael Ruse, *The Evolution-Creation Struggle* (Cambridge: Harvard University Press, 2005).

its turn, the Intelligent Design movement, with much more sophistication, still demonstrates a strong commitment to metaphysical univocity, harmonization, and natural theology, along with the use of modern probability theory and a tendency to treat the court of public opinion as a capable judge of controversial issues. Again, critics of Creation Science and Intelligent Design, both believers and unbelievers, also often share some of these attitudes, especially those derived from metaphysical univocity, harmonization, and natural theology.

If what I have sketched here portrays the past with any accuracy, it should be clear that when conservative Bible-believers object to different aspects of modern science, they do so on the basis of assumptions as well as arguments. Often missing in those considerations, however, are direct appeals to the heart of the Christian faith as defined by the person and work of Christ. Coming back to that center offers a better way of discriminating more accurately between assumptions well grounded in solid theology and those that are not.

A Case Study: B. B. Warfield, *Concursus,* and Evolution

A case study that shows how profitable it can be to approach scientific issues with christological principles is provided by the career of Benjamin B. Warfield. In chapter 3, when discussing the doubleness of classical Christology, we saw how Warfield forcefully affirmed "this conjoint humanity and divinity [of Christ], within the limits of a single personality."[10] It was precisely this regard for the Chalcedonian definition of Christ's person and work that enabled Warfield to handle with relative ease the knotty questions about evolution that arose during his lifetime.

From his position at Princeton Theological Seminary, Warfield wrote steadily from the 1880s until shortly before his death in 1921 about many aspects of his era's developing evolutionary theories.[11]

10. See above, 47.

11. Most of these works are reprinted, with editorial introductions, in B. B. Warfield, *Evolution, Science, and Scripture: Selected Writings,* ed. Mark A. Noll and David N. Livingstone (Grand Rapids: Baker, 2000).

These writings included major essays devoted to Darwin's biography ("Charles Darwin's Religious Life" in 1888 and "Darwin's Arguments against Christianity" the next year); several substantial articles directly on evolution or related scientific issues ("The Present Day Conception of Evolution" in 1895, "Creation versus Evolution" in 1901, "On the Antiquity and Unity of the Human Race" in 1911, and "Calvin's Doctrine of Creation" in 1915); and many reviews of relevant books, some of them mini-essays in their own right.

In these works, Warfield repeatedly insisted on distinguishing among Darwin as a person, Darwinism as a cosmological theory, and evolution as a series of explanations about natural development. Of key importance was his willingness throughout a long career to accept the possibility (or even the probability) of evolution, while also denying Darwinism as a cosmological theory. In his mind, these discriminations were necessary in order properly to evaluate both the results of disciplined observation (science) and large-scale conclusions drawn from that science (theology or cosmology). Crucially, a christological perspective was prominent when he applied these discriminations to evolutionary theory.

For positioning Warfield properly on these subjects, it is also vital to stress a conjunction of his convictions that has been much less common since his day. Besides his openness toward evolution, that is, Warfield was also the ablest modern defender of the theologically conservative belief in the inerrancy of the Bible.

During the late nineteenth century when critical views of Scripture came to prevail in American universities, Warfield was as responsible as any other American for refurbishing the conviction that the Bible communicates revelation from God entirely without error. Warfield's formulation of biblical inerrancy, in fact, has even been a theological mainstay for recent "creationist" convictions about the origin of the earth.[12] Yet while he defended biblical inerrancy, Warfield was also a cautious, discriminating, but entirely candid pro-

---

12. For the direct use of Warfield on the inerrancy of Scripture, see John C. Whitcomb Jr. and Henry M. Morris, *The Genesis Flood: The Biblical Record and Its Scientific Implications* (Philadelphia: Presbyterian and Reformed, 1961), xx.

ponent of the possibility that evolution might offer the best way to understand the natural history of the earth and of humankind. On this score his views place him with more recent thinkers who maintain ancient trust in the Bible while also affirming the modern scientific enterprise and mainstream scientific conclusions.[13] Warfield did not simply assert these two views randomly, but he sustained them learnedly, as coordinate arguments.

In the course of his career, both Warfield's positions and his vocabulary did shift on the question of evolution. But they shifted only within a fairly narrow range. What remained constant was his adherence to a broad Calvinistic conception of the natural world — of a world that, even in its most physical aspects, reflected the wisdom and glory of God — and his commitment to the goal of harmonizing a sophisticated conservative theology and the most securely verified conclusions of modern science. To state once again his combination of positions, Warfield consistently rejected materialist or ateleological explanations for natural phenomena (explanations that he

13. For example, Bernard Ramm, *The Christian View of Science and Scripture* (Grand Rapids: Eerdmans, 1954); Russell L. Mixter, ed., *Evolution and Christian Thought Today* (Grand Rapids: Eerdmans, 1959); D. C. Spanner, *Creation and Evolution: Some Preliminary Considerations* (London: Falcon Books, 1966); Malcolm A. Jeeves, ed., *The Scientific Enterprise and Christian Faith* (Downers Grove, IL: InterVarsity, 1969); Donald M. MacKay, *The Clockwork Image: A Christian Perspective on Science* (Downers Grove, IL: InterVarsity, 1974); Thomas F. Torrance, *Christian Theology and Scientific Culture* (New York: Oxford University Press, 1981); Davis A. Young, *Christianity and the Age of the Earth* (Grand Rapids: Zondervan, 1982); Charles E. Hummel, *The Galileo Connection: Resolving Conflicts between Science and the Bible* (Downers Grove, IL: InterVarsity, 1986); J. C. Polkinghorne, *One World: The Interaction of Science and Theology* (Princeton: Princeton University Press, 1986); Howard J. Van Till, *The Fourth Day: What the Bible and the Heavens Are Telling Us about the Creation* (Grand Rapids: Eerdmans, 1986); John Houghton, *Does God Play Dice? A Look at the Story of the Universe* (Leicester, England: Inter Varsity Press, 1988); Philip Duce, *Reading the Mind of God: Interpretation in Science and Theology* (Leicester, England: Apollos, 1998); Alister McGrath, *The Foundations of Dialogue in Science and Religion* (Oxford: Blackwell, 1998); Francis Collins, *The Language of God: A Scientist Presents Evidence for Belief* (New York: Free Press, 2007); Denis O. Lamoureux, *Evolutionary Creation: A Christian Approach to Evolution* (Eugene, OR: Wipf and Stock, 2008); and Karl W. Giberson, *Saving Darwin: How to Be a Christian and Believe in Evolution* (New York: HarperOne, 2008).

usually associated with "Darwinism"), even as he just as consistently entertained the possibility that other kinds of evolutionary explanations, which avoided Darwin's rejection of divine agency, could satisfactorily explain the physical world.

In several of his writings, Warfield carefully distinguished three ways in which God worked in and through the physical world. The most important thing about these three ways is that Warfield felt each of them was compatible with the theology he found in an inerrant Bible, if each was applied properly to natural history and to the history of salvation. "Evolution" meant developments arising out of forces that God had placed inside matter at the original creation of the world-stuff, but that God also directed to predetermined ends by his providential superintendence of the world. At least in writings toward the end of his life, Warfield held that evolution in this sense was fully compatible with biblical understandings of the production of the human body. "Mediate creation" meant the action of God upon matter to bring something new into existence that could not have been produced by forces or energy latent in matter itself. He did not apply the notion of "mediate creation" directly in his last, most mature writings on evolution, but it may be that he expounded the concept as much to deal with miracles or other biblical events as for developments in the natural world.[14] The last means of God's action was "creation *ex nihilo*," which Warfield consistently maintained was the way that God made the original stuff of the world.

On questions relating to evolution, orthodox Christology became relevant when Warfield invoked the concept of *concursus*. By this term he meant the coexistence of two usually contrary conditions or realities. In speaking of the person of Christ he had used a closely related term, "conjoined." For broader intellectual purposes, the key was to apply the same sense of harmoniously conjoined spheres to other domains.

As we will see with somewhat more detail when taking up Chris-

14. Warfield deployed a similar vocabulary in a discussion of miracles that he published at about the same time; see "The Question of Miracles," in *The Bible Student* (March-June 1903), as reprinted in *The Shorter Writings of Benjamin B. Warfield*, vol. 2, ed. John E. Meeter (Nutley, NJ: Presbyterian and Reformed, 1973), 167-204.

tology in relation to Scripture, Warfield held that the biblical authors were completely human as they wrote the Scriptures, even as they enjoyed the full inspiration of the Holy Spirit.[15] This principle, grounded in Christology and exemplified in the Bible, was also his guide for positing an (evolutionary) approach to nature where all living creatures were thought to develop fully (with the exception of the original creation and the human soul) through "natural" means. Warfield's basic stance, expressed first about Christ and then extrapolated for Scripture, was a doctrine of providence that saw God working in and with, instead of as a replacement for, the processes of nature. Late in his career, this same stance also grounded Warfield's opposition to "faith healing." In his eyes, physical healing through medicine and the agency of physicians was as much a result of God's action (if through secondary causes) as the cures claimed as a direct result of divine intervention.[16] *Concursus* was as important and as fruitful for his views on evolution as it was for his theology as a whole. It was a principle he felt the Scriptures offered to enable humans both to approach the world fearlessly and to do so for the greater glory of God.

Warfield's strongest statement on evolution came in 1915 when he published a lengthy article on John Calvin's view of creation.[17] Although he never stated it in so many words, it is clear that the convictions he ascribed to Calvin were also his own. He summarizes what he read in Calvin: "It should scarcely be passed without remark that Calvin's doctrine of creation is, if we have understood it aright, for all except the souls of men, an evolutionary one." God had called the "indigested mass" into existence *ex nihilo,* with a full "promise and potency" of what was to develop from that mass. Yet, according to Warfield's summary of Calvin, "all that has come into being since — except the souls of men alone — has arisen as a modification of this

---

15. See below, 130-32.

16. See Warfield, *Counterfeit Miracles* (New York: Scribner, 1918).

17. For Warfield's complete essay, see "Calvin's Doctrine of the Creation," in *The Works of Benjamin B. Warfield,* vol. 5, *Calvin and Calvinism* (New York: Oxford University Press, 1931), 287-349. The quotations that follow are taken from Warfield, *Evolution, Science, and Scripture,* 308-9.

original world-stuff by means of the interaction of its intrinsic forces." Warfield went on to affirm a robust doctrine of providence, whereby "all the modifications of the world-stuff have taken place under the directly upholding and governing hand of God, and find their account ultimately in His will." Critically, however, he saw these later modifications taking place through "secondary causes." And once "secondary causes" were viewed as the means by which the original creation was modified, we have, according to Warfield, "not only evolutionism but pure evolutionism."

Warfield makes clear that Calvin did not himself explicitly embrace evolutionary theory since Calvin "had no conception" of "the interaction of forces by which the actual production of forms was accomplished." Thus, lacking the information provided by modern students of nature, Calvin did not advocate a "theory" of evolution. But, Warfield insists, he did teach "a doctrine of evolution" that pictures God as producing the material stuff of the world "out of nothing," but then "all that is not immediately produced out of nothing is therefore not created — but evolved." Warfield then translates Calvin's notion of "secondary causes" into what he defines as "intrinsic forces." Warfield's summary repeats a second time: "And this, we say, is a very pure evolutionary scheme."

The point where Christology enters is where Warfield explains the deeper theology at work. In his summary, "Calvin's ontology of second causes was, briefly stated, a very pure and complete doctrine of *concursus,* by virtue of which he ascribed all that comes to pass to God's purpose and directive government." For readers of Warfield in the twenty-first century, it is frustrating that he did not go further in expounding on this theological basis. He does say that the "account" of how "secondary causes" work is "a matter of ontology; how we account for their existence, their persistence, their action — the relation we conceive them to stand in to God, the upholder and director as well as creator of them." But for his purposes with this essay, Warfield does not explore those ontological issues. The regret now is that, if he had taken up these ontological questions, he may have considered the Western tradition of univocity that had, in effect, dispensed with *concursus* in explaining the physical world.

As it is, we still have a most intriguing contribution to theology, science, and science considered in connection with theology. Warfield's discussion of Calvin on evolution certainly indicated that he thought his very high view of biblical inspiration was fully compatible with comprehensive forms of evolutionary science (as distinct from evolutionary cosmology). Whether Warfield interpreted Calvin correctly or not, whether Warfield understood correctly his era's scientific discoveries (in which he was well read for an amateur), or whether his own efforts at bringing together his era's scientific knowledge and his interpretation of the biblical record were correct — these are all important but secondary issues. The main point lies elsewhere. The Scriptures that Warfield trusted implicitly revealed a God to him who created the world, providentially superintended the world, and gave human beings the capacity to explain the world naturally (in terms of "secondary causes"). The key theological principle that enabled Warfield to draw these conclusions was his belief in the classical Christology of Nicea and Chalcedon.

Warfield's writings on evolution, the last of which appeared in the year of his death, 1921, cannot, of course, pronounce definitively on theological-scientific questions at the start of the twenty-first century. They can, however, show that sophisticated theology, nuanced argument, and careful sifting of scientific research are able to produce a much more satisfactory working relationship between science and theology than the heated strife that has dominated public debate on this subject since the time of Warfield's passing.

A Christology for Science

The theologian Robert Barron has nicely clarified much of what lies behind recent conflicts over human origins that feature supposedly biblical truths contending against supposedly scientific conclusions. In his words, "recent debates concerning evolutionist and 'creationist' accounts of the origins of nature are marked through and through by modern assumptions about a distant, competitive, and occasionally intervening God, whether the existence of such a God is affirmed

or denied."[18] Barron's response to these modern debates is a sophisticated exposition of classical Christology aimed at his theological
peers. My effort is much simpler and is aimed at academics in general, but it comes from the same christological perspective.

Christ as Creator, Sustainer, Redeemer

Classical Christian orthodoxy as expressed in the creeds that summarize the Scriptures begins at the beginning: nature owes its existence
to and is sustained by Jesus Christ. From this starting point several
important ramifications follow naturally.

One is the implication that the best way of finding out about nature is to look at nature. This implication comes directly from the
christological principle of contingency (see above, 49-55). As described in the Gospels, individuals who wanted to learn the truth
about Jesus had to "come and see." Likewise, to find out what might
be true in nature, it is necessary to "come and see."

The process of "coming and seeing" does not lead to infallible
truth about the physical world since there is no special inspiration
from the Holy Spirit for the Book of Nature as there is for the Book of
Scripture. But "coming and seeing" is still the method that belief in
Christ as Savior privileges for learning about all other objects, including nature. This privileging means that scientific results coming from
thoughtful, organized, and carefully checked investigations of natural phenomena must, for Christ-centered reasons, be taken seriously.

From this perspective, the successes of modern science in recent centuries testify implicitly to the existence of a creating and redeeming God. To once again quote Robert Barron, scientific activity

---

18. Robert Barron, *The Priority of Christ: Toward a Postliberal Catholicism* (Grand
Rapids: Brazos, 2007), 221. For convenience, I return several times in the following
paragraphs to this book by Robert Barron. But there are other parallel efforts, for example, from the physicist and Anglican theologian John C. Polkinghorne, in books like *Belief in God in an Age of Science* (New Haven: Yale University Press, 1998) and *Science and
the Trinity: The Christian Encounter with Reality* (New Haven: Yale University Press,
2004).

by its very nature "implies . . . an unavoidable correspondence between the activity of the mind and the structure of being: intelligence will find its fulfillment in this universal and inescapable intelligibility." But how can this implication be justified? According to Barron, "the universality of objective intelligibility (assumed by any honest scientist) can be explained only through recourse to a transcendent subjective intelligence that has thought the world into being, so that every act of knowing a worldly object or event is, literally, a recognition, a thinking again of what has already been thought by a primordial divine knower."[19] In lay language, the "transcendent subjective intelligence" and the "primordial divine knower" guarantee the possibility that a researcher's mind can grasp something real about the world beyond the mind. The Scriptures — in John 1, Colossians 1, and Hebrews 1 — provide a name for that "intelligence" and that "knower." In these terms, the existence of nature and the possibility of understanding nature presuppose Jesus Christ.

A second implication arising from the centrality of Christ in creation concerns the interpretation of Scripture. Classic biblical texts about the purpose of the Bible reinforce the foundational principle that the believers' confidence in Scripture rests on its message of salvation in Jesus Christ. Thus, in John 20, the Gospel story has been written down so "that you may believe that Jesus is the Christ, the Son of God, and that by believing you may have life in his name" (20:31). In 2 Timothy 3, the inspired or God-breathed "holy scriptures" have as their main purpose instruction "for salvation through faith in Christ Jesus" (3:15). And in 2 Peter 1, "the word of the prophets made more certain" as these prophets were "carried along by the Holy Spirit" (1:19, 21) deals preeminently with "the power and coming of our Lord Jesus Christ" (1:16).

As these passages suggest, salvation in Christ anchors the believer's confidence that all of Scripture is trustworthy.[20] But because of that supreme fact, the effort to understand *how* Scripture is trustworthy for questions like the ordering of nature should never stray far

19. Barron, *The Priority of Christ,* 154.
20. See above on providence, 30-33.

from consideration of Christ and his work. Yet as we have seen, "Christ and his work" includes, as an object, the material world of creation, and as a method, "come and see." In other words, following the Christ revealed in Scripture as Redeemer means following the Christ who made it possible for humans to understand the physical world and offered a means ("come and see") for gaining that understanding.

Final and ultimate disharmony between what "come and see" demonstrates about Christ and what "come and see" reveals about the world of nature is impossible. This Christ is the same one through whom God has worked "to reconcile to himself all things . . . making peace through his blood, shed on the cross" (Col. 1:20) and in whom "all things were created" and in whom "all things hold together" (1:16-17).

Yet it is indisputable that on some science-theology questions, trust in Christ (and therefore trust in Scripture) has seemed to conflict with trusting in what Christ-authorized procedure ("come and see") reveals about a Christ-created and Christ-sustained world. The parade of difficult questions arising from the effort to bring together standard interpretations of Scripture and standard interpretations of the natural world is a long one. Trying to answer these questions has been a consistent feature of the modern scientific age.

- In the nineteenth century, many earnest believers were wondering, if "coming and seeing" in geology and astronomy led to the conclusion that material existence has a very long history, should the "days" of Genesis 1 be understood as long periods of time or should a new interpretation of Genesis 1:1 be adopted that posits a "gap" between "in the beginning" and "God created"?
- More recent advances in both historical understanding (the ancient Near East) and empirical science (genetics, biology, astronomy) have prompted questions about the creation accounts of early Genesis. Well-trained scientists with strong Christian convictions have followed the Christ-rooted procedure of "coming and seeing" in their study of physical evidence for the origin of the universe and have concluded that much of standard evolu-

119

tionary theory seems well grounded.[21] Similarly, well-trained biblical scholars with strong Christian convictions have followed the Christ-rooted procedure of "coming and seeing" in their study of ancient Near Eastern cultures and have concluded that the early chapters of Genesis seem to be directly concerned about attacking idol-worship that substituted the sun or the moon for God.[22] Given the combination of these two streams of testimony, should it be thought that early Genesis is not concerned with modern scientific questions but is very much concerned about encouraging worship of the one true God who is the originator and sustainer of all things?

- Even more recently, the rough consensus on evolutionary change assembled from many scientific disciplines makes for even more complex questions: for example, if human evolution seems indicated by a wide range of responsible scientific procedures ("come and see"), how might responsible biblical interpretation understand the New Testament stress on Christ (very definitely in historical time and historical space) as overcoming the sinfulness inherited from Adam and Eve, whom Scripture, at least on a surface level, also represents as individuals in historical time and historical space?

All such questions caused understandable consternation when they were first raised, since they challenged specific interpretations of Scripture that had been tightly interwoven with basic interpretations of the entire Bible. Even after long and hard thought, such questions continue to pose definite challenges.

---

21. "The BioLogos Forum: Science and Faith in Dialogue" is a portal with much discussion of such research; see www.biologos.com.

22. For example, Derek Kidner, *Genesis: An Introduction and Commentary* (Downers Grove, IL: InterVarsity, 1967); Henri Blocher, *In the Beginning: The Opening Chapters of Genesis* (Downers Grove, IL: InterVarsity, 1984); Meredith G. Kline, "Space and Time in the Genesis Cosmogony," *Perspectives on Science and Christian Faith* 48 (1996): 2-15; Bruce K. Waltke and Cathi J. Fredricks, *Genesis: A Commentary* (Grand Rapids: Zondervan, 2001); and John H. Walton, *The Lost World of Genesis One: Ancient Cosmology and the Origins Debate* (Downers Grove, IL: InterVarsity, 2009).

Answering such questions responsibly requires sophistication in scientific knowledge and sophistication in biblical interpretation — exercised humbly, teachably, and nondefensively. Unfortunately, these traits and capacities have not always predominated when such questions are addressed. But the difficult questions will almost certainly only continue to multiply because of two ongoing realities: the Holy Spirit continues to bestow new life in Christ through the message of the cross found in Scripture, and responsible investigations lead plausibly to further evolutionary conclusions from the relevant scientific disciplines.

A Chalcedonian Perspective

The multiplication and intensification of such questions are, however, no cause for despair. For those with Christ these questions present instead a golden opportunity for returning to first principles. Almost the very first of those first principles is the Chalcedonian definition of Christ as fully divine and fully human in one integrated person.

If the mystery of divinity and humanity fully inhabiting a single being is at the heart of Christian faith, and if this faith offers Christ as the definite answer to the deepest mysteries of existence itself, then there is a way forward. It is not a way forward along the path of late-medieval univocity when it was assumed that a natural explanation for any phenomenon was a fully sufficient explanation. It is not a way forward along the path of William Paley's natural theology where it is assumed that humans may have God-like knowledge about the final purpose of physical phenomena. And it is not a way forward that either trivializes the Scriptures or distrusts modern science for ideological reasons. It is instead a way forward that tries to give both the study of nature its proper due as made possible because of Christ's creating work, and the interpretation of Scripture its proper due as revealing the mercy of redemption in Christ.

On specific questions concerning evolution, promising recent suggestions resting on classical Christology have come from Catholic scientists and theologians who draw on the insights of Thomas Aquinas. In particular, Thomas resisted the push toward univocity as he defended the complexity of the divine-human mystery at the heart of the universe. In his own day, as we have seen, Duns Scotus treated God and humanity as existing on a common metaphysical plane; God was infinitely greater than humans, but in quantity, not quality. No, said Thomas Aquinas, since humans are creatures and the triune God was the creator, humanity and deity do not share the same metaphysical plane. Hence, there must always be separation between human knowledge about existence and divine knowledge. Robert Barron states Thomas's position carefully: "Aquinas maintained consistently throughout his career that God is inescapably mysterious to the human intellect, since our frame of reference remains the creaturely mode of existence, which bears only an analogical resemblance to the divine mode of being. . . . The 'cash value' of the claim that God exists is that there is a finally mysterious source of the to-be of finite things."[23]

One of the payoffs in the twenty-first century from this thirteenth-century insight is relevant to debates about evolution, where the consensus in several scientific specialties posits a key role for "randomness" in describing physical changes over time. Thomas Aquinas offered what amounts to a prescient response when he described the contingency of much that transpires in the world (his contingency may be taken as roughly our randomness): "The effect of divine providence is not only that things should happen somehow, but that they should happen either by necessity or by contingency. Therefore, whatsoever divine providence ordains to happen infallibly and of necessity happens infallibly and of necessity; and that happens from contingency, which the divine providence conceives to happen from contingency."[24] God, in other words, never works capriciously, even though some providentially determined actions may look to humans like pure contingency. The metaphysical difference between God and humanity explains this difference in perspective.

---

23. Barron, *The Priority of Christ*, 13.

24. *A Summa of the Summa*, ed. Peter Kreeft (San Francisco: Ignatius, 1990), 174 (from Thomas Aquinas, *Summa Theologica* I.22.4).

A very recent Catholic statement has applied this type of reasoning to arguments between those who advocate Intelligent Design and those defending a purely unguided evolutionism. According to its authors, because this debate concerns "whether the available data support inferences of design or chance," the debate "cannot be settled by theology." That is to say, when empirical results are in view, the way to solve the questions is to "come and see." But the statement goes on with sophisticated attention to broader contexts: "It is important to note that, according to the Catholic understanding of divine causality, true contingency in the created order is not incompatible with a purposeful divine providence. Divine causality and created causality radically differ in kind and not only in degree. Thus, even the outcome of a truly contingent natural process can nonetheless fall within God's providential plan for creation."[25] Questions of chance and randomness exist on two levels, the empirical and the philosophical/theological. Each level deserves its own serious attention.

Under the assumptions promoted by medieval univocity, early modern theories of harmonizing Scripture and nature, and natural theology in the era of the Enlightenment, it has become customary to think that scientifically demonstrated randomness in nature counts as knockdown evidence against the existence of God. But this is both a logical and an ontological error. As phrased recently by the philosopher Alvin Plantinga, it is a logical error to move from asserting, "We know of no irrefutable objections to its being biologically possible that all of life has come to be by way of unguided Darwinian processes," to concluding: "All of life has come to be by way of unguided Darwinian processes."[26] It is an ontological error for the same reason that it is erroneous to think that if Jesus hungered and thirsted, he could not be the Son of God.

---

25. The Roman Curia: Pontifical Commissions, "Communion and Stewardship: Human Persons Created in the Image of God" (July 23, 2004); published in *La Civiltà Cattolica,* 2004, I, 254-86. Available on the Web at www.vatican.va/roman_curia/congregations/cfaith/cti_documents/rc_con_cfaith_doc_20040723_communion-stewardship_en.html (accessed May 18, 2010).

26. Alvin Plantinga, "The Dawkins Delusion," *Books & Culture,* March/April 2007, 22.

Satisfactory resolution of problems stemming from responsible biblical interpretation brought together with responsible interpretations of nature will not come easily. Such resolution requires more sophistication in scientific knowledge, more sophistication in biblical hermeneutics, and more humility of spirit than most of us possess. But it is not wishful thinking to believe that such resolution is possible. It is rather an expectant hope that grows directly from confidence in what has been revealed in Jesus Christ. If, therefore, humbly responsible thinkers, properly equipped scientifically and hermeneutically, conclude that the full picture of human evolution now standard in many scientific disciplines fits with a trustworthy interpretation of Scripture, that conclusion can be regarded as fully compatible with historic Christian orthodoxy as defined by the normative creeds.

SEVEN

Christology: The Foundation of Biblical Study

—◈◈◈—

He suffered and was buried and rose up on the third day in accordance with the Scriptures . . .

This chapter takes up issues of great complexity, and often much controversy, concerning how best to understand the Scriptures. Because of how central these questions have been for American evangelical Protestants, it is the chapter in the book with the tightest focus on this strand of Christian believers. Yet if the chapter is written particularly for evangelicals, my hope is that readers from other Christian traditions may also find it helpful for their own efforts at understanding, internalizing, and acting upon the written revelation from God.

The main point, however, is the same as in the chapters on history and science: for serious intellectual efforts, those who look to Christ as their prophet, priest, and king act most faithfully when they carry out those efforts with norms defined by Christ. The circularity of this reasoning when applied to Scripture is obvious, since the Bible tells us of Christ from whom we are to take our bearings when approaching Scripture. But in this case it is a propitious circularity.

The approach in this chapter is first to draw on the creeds once again for general orientation, then to use the writings of J. I. Packer for underscoring the importance of Scripture for evangelicals. The chapter then returns to B. B. Warfield for another application of the principle of *concursus*, this time to Scripture. It concludes with assessments of arguments in a recent book that urged a Christ-centered approach in reading and interpreting the Scriptures.

The Bible in the Creeds

The summary of biblical teaching in the Apostles' Creed makes no direct mention of Scripture, though its affirmation of belief in the Holy Spirit can be read as an indirect reference. In the Nicene Creed as expanded in 381, there is only one brief reference, but it is crucial for how it is placed to highlight the work of redemption. According to the creed, the Lord Jesus Christ "was crucified on our behalf under Pontius Pilate; he suffered and was buried and rose up on the third day in accordance with the Scriptures."[1] The same sort of brief, but central, reference comes at the end of the Chalcedonian Definition of Christ's person. As it brought that definition to a close, the council affirmed that it had provided this doctrinal summary "just as the prophets taught from the beginning about him [the same only-begotten Son, God, Word, Lord Jesus Christ], and as the Lord Jesus Christ instructed us, and as the creed of the fathers [Nicea] handed it down to us."[2]

The creeds were never intended to be a comprehensive survey of all biblical wisdom. But by their explicit references to Scripture as revealing the great work of God in Christ, Nicea and Chalcedon do make an indirect assertion about the primary function of the Bible. Beyond its many other necessary uses, Scripture has been given primarily to communicate the story of the divine kingdom inaugurated in, by, with, and under Jesus Christ.

1. *Creeds and Confessions of Faith in the Christian Tradition*, ed. Jaroslav Pelikan and Valerie Hotchkiss, 3 vols. (New Haven: Yale University Press, 2003), 1:163.
2. *Creeds and Confessions*, 1:181.

Evangelicals and the Bible

The evangelical traditions, which take their name from the "good news" *(evangel)* about Christ, have always considered Scripture the norm above all norms. On this Biblio-centrism, it is appropriate to quote J. I. Packer, who has done so much over the last half-century to defend the God-given authority of Scripture.[3] It is also striking to note the analogy between Christ and Scripture with which he began a recent statement:

> Evangelicals maintain that as God has enthroned his Son, the living Word, as Lord of the universe, so he has enthroned the Bible, his written word, as the means of Christ's rule over the consciences of his disciples. The 66-book Protestant canon is held to be divinely inspired and authoritative, true and trustworthy, informative and imperative, life-imparting and strength-supplying to the human heart, and to be given to the church to be preached, taught, expounded, applied, absorbed, digested and appealed to as arbiter whenever questions of faith and life, belief and behavior, spiritual wisdom and spiritual welfare, break surface among the saints. Of the unifying bonds of evangelicalism, this view and use of Scripture is the strongest of all.[4]

Such definite statements about the foundation of evangelical Christianity in Scripture have sometimes been understood, by evangelicals and observers of evangelicals alike, to imply a negative — that because the Bible has supreme importance, nothing else can be important. This negative inference is an unfortunate error, not least for shortchanging "Christ's rule" to which Packer refers.

Most importantly, it is only fitting that believers in the Bible should guide their use of the Bible by what the Bible has to say about

---

3. For example, J. I. Packer, *"Fundamentalism" and the Word of God* (Grand Rapids: Eerdmans, 1958); *God Speaks to Man: Revelation and the Bible* (Philadelphia: Westminster, 1965); and *God's Words* (Grand Rapids: Baker, 1981).

4. J. I. Packer, "The Bible in Use: Evangelicals Seeking Truth from Holy Scripture," in *Your Word Is Truth,* ed. Richard John Neuhaus and Charles Colson (Grand Rapids: Eerdmans, 2002), 62-63.

itself. Yet biblical statements about the Bible, while they stress the utter truthfulness of Scripture, do not claim that the Scriptures are intended to adjudicate directly all questions of human learning and human social organization. So it is with the classic statement that we have already cited from the Gospel of John: "these [things about Jesus] are written that you may believe that Jesus is the Christ, the Son of God, and that by believing you may have life in his name" (John 20:31). And the equally classic statement in the Second Epistle to Timothy: "from infancy you have known the holy Scriptures, which are able to make you wise for salvation through faith in Christ Jesus. All Scripture is God-breathed and is useful for teaching, rebuking, correcting and training in righteousness, so that the man of God may be thoroughly equipped for every good work" (2 Tim. 3:15-17). The emphasis in these classic passages was well caught in 1974 by the Lausanne Covenant, the twentieth century's most widely used evangelical statement of faith: "We affirm the divine inspiration, truthfulness and authority of both Old and New Testament Scriptures in their entirety as the only written Word of God, without error in all that it affirms, and the only infallible rule of faith and practice. We also affirm the power of God's Word to accomplish his purpose of salvation."[5]

The Bible's story may indeed be considered a metanarrative subsuming all other narratives, or a truth that relativizes all other forms of knowledge. But as metanarrative and final truth, the Bible does not speak directly about everything per se. It rather speaks of everything indirectly, because it speaks of the origin, redemption, and final purpose of all things. Believing what the Bible says about the Bible, in other words, makes it possible to affirm both that the Bible provides a comprehensively true perspective on all things and that the Bible does not explain everything in the world directly. With the Scriptures' own statements about themselves in view, attitudes toward studying the world — eagerness to exploit secondary ways of knowing — should be opened up rather than shut down. This openness to experi-

5. *The Lausanne Covenant,* edited and commentary by John Stott (Minneapolis: World Wide Publications, 1975), 10.

encing the world, in turn, is exactly what a biblical vision of divine creation, with Christ as the active agent, encourages.

Accidents of history, rather than anything intrinsically biblical, have left the false impression among evangelicals that statements about the Bible imply a negative stance toward other forms of knowledge.[6] Once again, it is appropriate to quote J. I. Packer on the mistaken inference that trust in the Bible necessitates mistrust of either Christian traditions or human learning in general.

> On a sadder note, evangelical emphasis on the Bible has often led to the neglect of other important elements of Christian thought. It has meant evangelical isolation from the mainstream Christian heritage of Bible-based theology and wisdom over two millennia, which evangelicals should claim but which few seem to know or care about; from evangelicalism's own heritage of theology and exposition, which most simply ignore; and from the searchings and findings of the physical, historical, and human sciences, with their never-ending quests to push out further the walls of human knowledge.[7]

In Packer's phrase, "*sola scriptura* was never meant to imply that what is not mentioned in the Bible is not real, or is unimportant and not worth our attention, or that the history of biblical exegesis and exposition, and of theological construction and confession, over two millennia, need not concern us today, or that we should restrict our interest in God's world and in the arts, sciences, products, and dreams of our fellow-human beings." Rather, "The Bible has been given us, not to define for us the realities of the created order, nor to restrain our interests in them, but to enable us to diagnose, understand, appreciate, and handle them as we meet them, so that we may use and enjoy them to the Creator's praise."[8]

For a truly biblical view of the Bible, it is important not to treat

---

6. Describing these historical accidents was a main concern of *The Scandal of the Evangelical Mind.*

7. Packer, "The Bible in Use," 76-77.

8. Packer, "The Bible in Use," 77-78.

the Bible as a storehouse of information sufficient in itself for all things but to embrace, rather, the Bible's own perspective that leads its readers to a God-ordained openness to all things.

Reprise: B. B. Warfield and *Concursus*

We have already seen how the conservative Presbyterian theologian B. B. Warfield explained the person of Christ as "conjoint humanity and divinity, within the limits of a single personality,"[9] and then how he relied upon a similar notion of *concursus* to adjudicate the relationship of biological evolution and divine providence.[10] In his many writings on Scripture, reliance on the same concept played a major role.[11] Most importantly for our purposes, Warfield's exposition of the inerrancy of the Bible led him to affirm the fully human character of Scripture alongside its fully divine character. His reasoning, thus, offers a telling example of how a cast of mind shaped by meditation on the Trinity, the general purposes of God, and the work of Christ came into play when he thought about the Scriptures specifically.

A short essay from 1894, "The Divine and Human in the Bible," shows how fruitfully an underlying conception of *concursus* could function for questions concerning the Bible.[12] In this essay Warfield attacked zero-sum notions of biblical inspiration, where the divine and human aspects of Scripture are considered "as lying over against each other, dividing the Bible between them; or, as factors in inspiration, as striving against and excluding each other, so that where one enters the other is pushed out." The difficulty with such zero-sum reasoning was

---

9. See above, 47.

10. See above, 110-16.

11. Many of those writings are collected in *The Works of Benjamin B. Warfield*, vol. 1, *Revelation and Inspiration* (Grand Rapids: Baker, 1981; original 1927).

12. "The Divine and Human in the Bible," *Presbyterian Journal*, May 3, 1894. The quotations here are from the reprinting of the article in B. B. Warfield, *Selected Shorter Writings*, vol. 2, ed. John E. Meeter (Phillipsburg, NJ: Presbyterian and Reformed, 1973), 545-48. The article is also reprinted in B. B. Warfield, *Evolution, Science, and Scripture*, ed. Mark A. Noll and David N. Livingstone (Grand Rapids: Baker, 2000), 51-58.

illustrated by the mistaken conclusion "that every discovery of a human trait in Scripture is a disproving of the divinity of Scripture. If, then, it be discovered that the whole fabric of the Bible is human — as assuredly is true — men who start with this conception in mind must end with denying of the whole fabric of the Bible that it is divine."

By contrast, when Warfield turned to consider the right way of approaching the problem, he drew on reasoning shaped by his Christology: "Justice is done to neither factor of inspiration and to neither element in the Bible, the human or the divine, by any other conception of the mode of inspiration except that of *concursus,* or by any other conception of the Bible except that which conceives of it as a divine-human book, in which every word is at once divine and human." In explaining what he meant by *concursus,* Warfield referred to philosophy, as he did also in his comments on evolution. But in this discussion of Scripture he fleshed out that reference with a series of examples: "The philosophical basis of this conception is the Christian idea of God as immanent as well as transcendent in the modes of his activity. Its idea of the mode of the divine activity in inspiration is in analogy with the divine modes of activity in other spheres — in providence, and in grace wherein we work out our own salvation with fear and trembling, knowing that it is God who is working in us both the willing and the doing according to his own good pleasure." Thus, in Scripture, according to Warfield, are found "the constant . . . representation of the divine and human co-authorship of the Biblical commandments and enunciations of truth; as well as in the constant Scriptural ascription of Bible passages to both the divine and the human authors, and in the constant Scriptural recognition of Scripture as both divine and human in quality and character."

Although Warfield did not discuss the history of philosophy in this brief reference, he was clearly protesting against the iron grip that assumptions about univocity and crude notions of harmonization had fastened on Western thought. His restatement returned to something like a Presbyterian application of a Thomistic principle:

the whole of Scripture is the product of divine activities which enter it, however, not by superseding the activities of the human authors, but confluently with them; so that the Scriptures are the joint product of divine and human activities, both of which penetrate them at every point, working harmoniously together to the production of a writing which is not divine here and human there, but at once divine and human in every part, every word and every particular. . . . The human and divine factors in inspiration are conceived of as flowing confluently and harmoniously to the production of a common product. And the two elements are conceived of in the Scriptures as the inseparable constituents of one single and uncompounded product. . . . All the qualities of divinity and of humanity are to be sought and may be found in every portion and element of the Scripture.

Warfield brought his discussion to a close by quoting his contemporary Brooke Foss Westcott, the distinguished New Testament scholar and textual critic, and with his own summation. In both cases, the reasoning was directly parallel to the classical view of Christ who as human could enjoy full identification with human beings and as divine could effect their redemption: "'The Bible,' says Dr. Westcott, 'is authoritative, for it is the Word of God; it is intelligible, for it is the word of man.' Because it is the word of man in every part and element, it comes home to our hearts. Because it is the word of God in every part and element, it is our constant law and guide."

In the century and more since Warfield published these words, many others have also considered the character of Scripture as both an ordinary product of ordinary human processes and an extraordinary expression of extraordinary divine revelation. Discerning how to sort out the levels of theological reasoning at work has never been an easy task. One recent effort, however, has drawn unusual attention for making just such an effort.

Inspiration (of Scripture) and Incarnation (of Christ)

Peter Enns's recent book, *Inspiration and Incarnation: Evangelicals and the Problem of the Old Testament,* has been a source of considerable controversy.[13] Not only did it lead to the loss of Enns's teaching position at Westminster Theological Seminary, but it has also stimulated much published and online commentary.[14] My discussion of this book is not meant to endorse every one of its conclusions, but to say that Enns was moving in the right direction by trying to use the message of Scripture about Christ as the norm for understanding Scripture. A fully Christian way of approaching Scripture must certainly keep the incarnation of the Son of God fully in view.

Enns's first two proposals are the most important for our concerns because they feature the Christ-Scripture relationship directly. First is his appeal for what he calls *christotelic* biblical interpretation. He means by this phrase that each part of Scripture should be related to the grand story of Jesus Christ, who fulfills the purposes for which God both created the world and revealed himself through the Law and Prophets to Israel. To drive home this point, Enns does not quote the NT passages we have already cited (John 20:31; 2 Tim. 3:16; 2 Pet. 1:16-22). He draws on Jesus' words to the two disciples on the road to Emmaus from Luke 24:44-45 to establish what Enns calls "a hermeneutical foundation of how the Old Testament is now to be understood by Christians" (119): "[Jesus] said to them, 'This is what I told you while I was still with you: Everything must be fulfilled that is written about me in the Law of Moses, the Prophets and the Psalms.' Then he opened their minds so they could understand the Scriptures." In this first goal, Enns is urging his fellow evangelicals to be gospel-oriented in their hermeneutical and exegetical understanding.

Enns's second goal echoes the shape of B. B. Warfield's thinking by advocating "the incarnational *parallel* between Christ and the Bi-

13. Peter Enns, *Inspiration and Incarnation: Evangelicals and the Problem of the Old Testament* (Grand Rapids: Baker, 2005). Page numbers from this volume are enclosed in parentheses in the text.

14. Ted Olsen, "Westminster Theological Seminar Suspends Peter Enns," ChristianityTodayliveblog, March 27, 2008; http://blog.christianitytoday.com/ctliveblog/archives/2008/03/westminster_the.html (accessed May 5, 2010). For careful responses to Enns's proposals, see Bruce Waltke (with a rejoinder from Enns included), "Revisiting *Inspiration and Incarnation*," *Westminster Theological Journal* 71 (Spring 2009): 83-128, and G. K. Beale, *The Erosion of Inerrancy in Evangelicalism: Responding to New Challenges to Biblical Authority* (Wheaton, IL: Crossway, 2008).

ble" (168). He contends that believers should affirm about the Bible what the Christian church has long affirmed about Jesus Christ, that he was (in the words of the Chalcedonian Definition) "perfect in divinity and perfect in humanity, the same truly God and truly man, of a rational soul and a body; consubstantial with the Father as regards his divinity, and the same consubstantial with us as regards his humanity." Or as Enns puts it, "The long-standing identification between Christ the word and Scripture the word is central to how I think through the issues raised in this book: How does Scripture's full humanity and full divinity affect what we should expect from Scripture?" (18). In his treatment Enns, however, goes beyond Warfield by being very specific about how he thinks the analogy between the incarnate Christ and the enscripturated revelation should function.

Enns's third goal is to argue for using the Bible's own interpretive practices and assumptions as keys for constructing a biblical hermeneutic today. This goal takes Enns into the book's three case studies, which he explores as a way of urging contemporary interpreters of the Bible to self-consciously follow scriptural procedures as they set about their reading, understanding, preaching, and teaching Scripture.

Enns's fourth goal is the converse of the third. He is convinced that evangelicals in particular have imbibed a very strong dose of intellectual modernism as they have labored to defend the integrity of Scripture against the conclusions of secular modernists. In his account, modernism means accepting standards of scientific rationality aimed at producing verifiable clarity as measured by contemporary standards of authorial intention, verifiable historicity, ethical harmony, and grammatical-historical exegesis. Enns states this argument against evangelical modernism in many ways, for instance: "The problems many of us [evangelicals] feel regarding the Bible may have less to do with the Bible itself and more to do with our own preconceptions" (15). Again, when he describes the moves of theological conservatives against critics who read the Old Testament (OT) as merely reflecting the ethical norms and standards of historiography of ancient Near Eastern cultures, Enns claims to see the same kind of intellectual modernism at work among the conservatives as in their secular opponents: "The conservatives' reaction was also problematic in that it implicitly assumed what their opponents also assumed: the Bible, being the word of God, ought to be historically accurate in all its details (since God would not lie or make errors) and unique in its own setting (since God's word is revealed, which implies a specific type of uniqueness)." The problem is that "conservative scholarship, allowing modern scholarship to set the agenda[,] [was] still trying to maintain older doctrinal commitments" despite what legitimate evidence might reveal. Again, the problem was preconceived commitments overriding "the historical evidence that challenged doctrine" (47). In short, Enns perceives modernism at work among evangelicals whenever they use doctrinal assumptions about what the Bible has to mean and how the Bible must be interpreted to override what carefully sifted research shows about Scripture. Enns wants such modernism replaced by self-conscious reliance on interpretations and interpretive principles taken from Scripture itself.

Like Warfield, Enns is not interested in issues of philosophical background. But if he were, his appeal to trusting both the divine truthfulness of Scripture and the most reliable conclusions of research into the nature of biblical writings would sound familiar. It bears, that is, strong similarity to arguments about seeking harmony between Scripture and science not in the details but in foundational reflections on how an infinite deity relates to a finite world.

While the devil is definitely in the details when it comes to arguments like Enns's, it is not a stretch to think that biblically minded theological traditionalists should approve of his overarching goal of being biblical when interpreting the Bible. There is also every reason for concluding that the Bible should be considered as preeminently the story of salvation where "in the past God spoke to our forefathers through the prophets at many times and in various ways, but in these last days he has spoken to us by his Son, whom he appointed heir of all things, and through whom he made the universe" (Heb. 1:1-2). In addition, it is also clear that understanding how divine and human coexist in the written Word should comport with the reality of divine and human in the living Word. If the Bible is the guide for *what* we believe, it should certainly also be the guide for how we *use* the Bible to determine what we believe. With the apostle Paul's injunction in mind — "Do not conform any longer to the pattern of this world, but be transformed by the renewing of your mind" (Rom. 12:2) — it may be proper for Bible believers to exploit the intellectual resources of modernity, but certainly never proper to be captured by the intellectual assumptions of modernity.

Enns, of course, is not just stating principles. He devotes most of his book to three case studies designed to show what his principles mean in practice. Proper adjudication of the cases must remain for those with the necessary expertise. Yet taking Enns's examples seriously is important. Far too often, "Christian scholarship" remains abstract. Because Enns has taken his discussion into concrete cases, the cases deserve careful attention. Moreover, if believing scholars reject the conclusions he has drawn, their duty is then to show how alternative conclusions may be anchored even more securely in even more comprehensive understandings of the general purposes of the Bible.

Enns's first case study asks how the OT is to be understood against the background of ancient Near Eastern literature. Here his incarnational point is that if we worship Jesus Christ as God appearing as a human in the culture of first-century Palestine, then we must study God's revelation to ancient Israel by understanding the conventions of ancient Near Eastern cultures. Practically, in Enns's view, this incarnational strategy means simply accepting the fact that OT revelation inevitably reflected assumptions present in ancient cultures about cosmology, ethics, and historicity that are often at odds with modern assumptions.

As a prime example, Enns focuses on Abraham: "God adopted Abraham as the forefather of a new people, and in doing so he also adopted the mythic categories within which Abraham — and everyone else — thought" (53). In other words, to understand the stories about Abraham in Genesis *biblically,* it is necessary to reconstruct how Abraham would have thought. But to understand how Abraham would have thought means taking seriously what is gained from study of older contemporary texts like *Enuma Elish,* Atrahasis, Gilgamesh, and the Code of Hammurabi. Once this incarnational step is taken — that is, to enter into the Pentateuch with the mind-set that God put to use when he inspired the writing of the Pentateuch — several interpretative conclusions are obvious. For example, the Pentateuch is not primarily intended as a modern text on Near Eastern history. Rather, in Enns's words, "The reason the biblical account is different from its ancient Near Eastern counterparts is not that it is history in the modern sense of the word and therefore divorced from any similarity to ancient Near Eastern myth. What makes Genesis different from its ancient Near Eastern counterparts is that it begins to make the point to Abraham and his seed that the God they are bound to, the God who called them into existence, is different from the gods around them" (53). It, therefore, follows that understanding the Pentateuch aright means postponing the effort to answer characteristically modern questions (no matter how pressing they may seem) in order to grasp what the revelation to Abraham and his descendants primarily meant — first to them and therefore also to the latter-day children of Abraham grafted into his progeny by the gracious acts of God in Christ. As a specific example of this strategy, "It is a fundamental misunderstanding of Genesis to expect it to answer questions generated by a modern worldview, such as whether the days were literal or figurative, or whether the days of creation can be lined up with modern science, or whether the flood was local or universal. The question that Genesis is prepared to answer is whether Yahweh, the God of Israel, is worthy of worship" (55).

In considering the relation of Scripture to Near Eastern literature, Enns also addresses the thorny question of historicity. "Historicity" here is the issue of how to interpret historical-appearing materials that, if read in a newspaper today, would elicit as our first question: Does the account we have read reflect what actually happened? Enns treats the issue of "historicity" by comparing the parallel accounts of Israel's history in Samuel-Kings and the Chronicles. He argues that our instinctive modern reaction should not give us the first question when approaching these texts. Rather, we should move, first, from our acceptance of the phenomena of Scripture as revelation given by God to, second, discover the purposes that the phenomena of Scripture were intended to serve and, third, to make conclusions about what Scripture is teaching.

By following this procedure, Enns comes to these conclusions about the books of Samuel, Kings, and Chronicles: since we start with the fact of "*two different* accounts of virtually the same historical period" (63), we must ask why we have two differing accounts. Study of relevant OT contexts (for example, the placement of Chronicles as the last book in the Hebrew Bible) leads inevitably to the conclusion that "Chronicles was probably not written merely to supplement Samuel-Kings. Rather it is an independent piece of historiography . . . intended to stand on its own and be understood in its own terms." Since Samuel-Kings was written to describe why Israel was sent into exile, and Chronicles was written to describe what Israel should do after being in exile, it is only natural that the former features the decline and fall of David's house while the latter features the general purposes of God for an apparently abandoned people. If, however, we in our modern age are obsessed with questions about how to harmonize what look to us like the factual statements of Samuel-Kings with the factual statements of Chronicles, we miss the point. Those are our problems, but not the problems of the biblical authors. Or in Enns's terms, "The plain fact of the matter is that in Scripture we have two divergent accounts of the same event. The only question before us is how to handle this fact with integrity" (65).

As he concludes his treatment of the OT in relation to its surrounding cultures, Enns restates his *christotelic* theme: when we align our questions with what we discover the OT was trying to do, we can only conclude that the purpose of the OT was to begin "a larger story that God brings to an end many hundreds of years later in Christ" (67). Interpretive conclusions, interpretive techniques, interpretive assumptions, and interpretive conflicts that miss this main point are, according to Enns, instances of modernism elbowing aside God's own purposes for the Scriptures.

Enns's second case study treats theological and ethical diversity in the OT. In a word, Enns is not worried about many of the staple interpretive conundrums of the last two and a half centuries: Why do the two versions of the Ten Commandments differ in details? Why does God condemn convictions in Job's friends that the Lord's prophets encourage generally in his people? Why do regulations governing Israel's slaves seem to conflict? Why are animal sacrifices described

138

as both essential and inessential? Why does God both scorn Gentiles and desire all Gentiles to be redeemed? Does God change his mind or not? And so on.

Despite the oceans of learned ink that have been spilled on such matters, Enns thinks they are mostly badly posed questions reflecting the intellectual pressures of modernity. They are, in his picture, largely irrelevant to the important deliverances of divine revelation. In this view both secularists who use such apparent discrepancies to show that the OT cannot be inspired and evangelicals who harmonize such discrepancies to prove that the OT is inspired are equally modernistic. Or as Enns puts it, "for modern evangelicalism the tendency is to move toward a defensive or apologetic handling of the biblical evidence, to protect the Bible against the modernist charge that diversity is evidence of errors in the Bible, and, consequently, that the Bible is not inspired by God. Unfortunately, this legacy accepts the worldview offered by modernity and defends the Bible by a rational standard that the Bible itself challenges rather than acknowledges" (108).

By contrast, according to Enns, the proper response to confessing the Bible as the Word of God is to shape assumptions about how to interpret the Bible by *beginning* with the Bible. So if we find ethical, theological, and historical diversity in Scripture, we *begin* with the assumption that what the Bible intends for us to learn is not primarily concerned with textual unity or precise moral consistency as construed by modern ethicists, theologians, and historians. Rather, "The unity of the Bible is more subtle but at the same time deeper. It is a unity that should ultimately be sought in Christ himself, the living Word. . . . It is . . . a broad and foundational theological commitment based on the analogy between Christ and Scripture" (110).

Enns's third case study examines the use that New Testament (NT) writers make of OT texts. Here he rushes through a series of problems that have been studied by many scholars, perhaps most impressively by evangelical scholars.[15] Enns appreciates their labors, but he

---

15. For example, Richard N. Longenecker, *Biblical Exegesis in the Apostolic Period,* 2nd ed. (Grand Rapids: Eerdmans, 1999); Richard Hays, *Echoes of Scripture in the Letters of Paul* (New Haven: Yale University Press, 1989); and G. K. Beale and D. A. Carson, *Commentary on the New Testament Use of the Old Testament* (Grand Rapids: Baker, 2007).

also feels that, even though they are fully aware of the historical con-texts in which NT authors wrote, they do not fully appreciate the impli-cations of how these authors use those conventions. The problem be-comes acute when it is realized that the conventions of textual interpretation used by NT authors differ substantially from the conven-tions of modern interpreters. The crux is how to interpret NT use of OT passages if that usage depends as much or more on conventions of Sec-ond Temple interpretive practice as upon a strict grammatical-historical understanding of the OT passages in question. (The Second Temple period extended from circa 500 B.C. to A.D. 70.) As an example, Enns looks at Paul's quotation of Isaiah 49:8 in 2 Corinthians 6:1-2: "As God's fellow workers we urge you not to receive God's grace in vain. For he says, 'In the time of my favor I heard you, / and in the day of salvation I helped you.' I tell you, now is the time of God's favor, now is the day of salvation" (135). Enns holds that Paul at this point is not interpreting Isaiah with the canons of "modern, scientific exegesis." In fact, Paul is using Isaiah here in ways that violate a grammatical-historical interpre-tation of the OT in order to carry out "an interpretive exercise founded on his conviction that Christ is the ultimate fulfillment of Isaiah's story" (135). It is similar with Enns's conclusions about Paul's discus-sion of the seed of Abraham, references by the author of Hebrews to Psalm 95, and even Jesus' statement in Luke 24 about "what is written" in the Law, the Prophets, and the Psalms. In each case, the NT usage fol-lows more the ancient practice of intertestamental authors and the Qumran scrolls than it does the modern canons of grammatical-historical exegesis. Enns's effort to treat NT uses of the OT in line with his general aim for the book is quite clear: "the important point is this: that 'original context matters' must be applied not only to *grammar* and *history* but also to the hermeneutics of the New Testament writers" (117, emphasis in original).

In my personal view, Enns is not as clear in this third case study as in the other two about how he feels contemporary biblical interpre-tation should move if it follows the norms of the NT writers in their use of the OT. On the one hand, he does not want evangelicals today bound completely to grammatical-historical interpretation, since he argues that this practice heeds intellectual modernism as much as it heeds the NT. On the other hand, he does not seem comfortable with contemporary interpretations that treat the OT with the typological or allegorical abandon that he finds in at least some NT uses of the OT. Again, however, his focus is on the Christ-centered purposes of NT revelation: "The New Testament is similar to other Second Temple texts in two respects: the interpretive methods used and the interpretive traditions they adopt. . . . [T]ime and again the New Testament authors do some odd things, by our standards, with the Old Testament, but these things can be explained by taking note of the interpretive context in which the New Testament writers lived" (152).

On the knotty issues at stake in this problem, Enns is most compelling when he explains NT practices on the analogy of the incarnation: "God gave us the gospel not as an abstract doctrinal formulation, but already contextualized. Revelation necessarily implies a human context. . . . For the apostles to interpret the Old Testament in ways consistent with the hermeneutical expectations of the Second Temple world is analogous to Christ himself becoming a Second Temple citizen" (160-61). Yet the reality that the NT's account of Jesus Christ brings OT accounts to their God-ordained conclusion does not offer much help to answering the question that Enns himself poses: "Should we handle the Old Testament the way the Apostles did?" (156). His concluding words in this discussion are certainly true: "The reality of the crucified and risen Christ is both the beginning and end of Christian biblical interpretation" (163). But those words do not go very far in helping exegetes, teachers, or preachers in their own efforts at showing specific connections between OT anticipations and NT fulfillment.

Taking Stock

The proposals that Peter Enns develops in *Inspiration and Incarnation* merit the closest scrutiny precisely for his effort to study Scripture with the Scriptures' main story of God and work in Christ as the guiding rubric. In response, the following conclusions or questions seem appropriate.

First, Enns's efforts at making biblical hermeneutics more biblical should be applauded by all evangelicals — indeed, by all Christians — even if it means rethinking many time-honored conclusions. If by taking advantage of new historical knowledge about ancient cultures and using techniques of literary and cultural analysis that have been developed to secure that knowledge, believers agree on some matters with secularists who deny the inspired character of Scripture, this is not automatically a bad thing. The key distinction is that believing scholars will use this knowledge and these techniques to clarify what biblical authors meant as a way of seeing more clearly what God has revealed. (I think this is what Enns means in desiring to extend grammatical-historical exegesis to grammatical-historical hermeneutics.) The imperative demand is that Christian scholars use this knowledge and these techniques for their own purposes, conforming neither to the anti-Christian assumptions of secularists who also use them, nor to the fears of evangelicals who hesitate to put them to use.

Second, at the same time, what Enns seeks would require more critical self-consciousness than most scholars have been able to tolerate. To be self-consciously more biblical in approaching Scripture means being more self-critically conscious about where assumptions shape intellectual labor in history, exegesis, and theology. Thus, as an evangelical historian, I would need to push myself to understand the religious and philosophical assumptions with which I approach my research. The same must be true for Christian exegetes and Christian theologians. Christian exegetes need to be probingly self-critical about the religious and philosophical foundations of grammatical-historical interpretation: Are exegetes able to say whether Enns is correct in labeling grammatical-historical interpretative principles as (at least sometimes) covert forms of modernism? Likewise, Christian theologians need to be probingly self-critical about the religious and philosophical foundations undergirding efforts to move beyond narrow fundamentalist or partisan sectarian approaches to theology: Are theologians able to say to an author like Enns that they are consistently striving to think in terms of the biblical story of creation-fall-redemption-kingdom, and not in terms set by modern or postmodern conventions?

Third, the analogy between the incarnation and the inspiration of Scripture is a fruitful one, though, as with all analogies, it is necessary to specify points of difference as well as points of alignment. For believers in the incarnation, adding to background knowledge of biblical writings can never substitute for apprehension of what God was accomplishing in Christ. It is a modernist mistake to believe that, as we come to understand more about what makes human cultures work and learn more about the actual shape of past human events, we must reduce what we ascribe to the actions of God in those cultures and events. It is a Christian response to believe that such increased knowledge can exist conjointly with increased confidence in God's actions, since in the incarnation we see a full demonstration of complete humanity and complete deity acting confluently for the redemption of the world.

Fourth, Enns's work has obvious implications for scholars trying to understand statements from Jesus in the Gospels about OT history, the authorship of OT books, and the bearing of OT moral standards for Christian ethics. If what Jesus said in his incarnate person partook fully of the particular cultural conventions in which "for us humans and for our salvation he came down from heaven and became incarnate" (Nicene Creed) — and it is necessary to make this affirmation in order to avoid the heresy of Docetism — then the primary meaning of such statements must be sought in what they affirm concerning the fulfillment of God's overall plan of salvation (creation-fall-Israel-Christ-church-end). The bearing of these statements on modern questions about OT history, OT authorship, and OT contributions to Christian ethics may still be sought, but only by researching the norms of interpretation that prevailed in first-century Palestine during the Second Temple period and then by asking what Jesus' statements couched in those Second Temple norms might tell us about questions of fact concerning OT history, OT authorship, and OT contributions to Christian ethics. To follow this line of reasoning would still provide considerable authoritative teaching from the OT, but not as much as evangelical interpreters have sometimes held Jesus to be offering.

Fifth, Enns's approach to questions of historicity is appealing for how it sails between the Charybdis of modernist positions (where every history-like assertion in the Bible must be judged errant or infallible depending on whether it can plausibly be matched with events that can be demonstrated to have occurred) and the Scylla of postmodern relativism (where all historical accounts are only the projection back onto the past of contemporary relations of power, contemporary ideologies, and contemporary philosophical conventions). Instead, Enns seems to follow the Scriptures in affirming the basic historical factuality of the main outlines of Abrahamic and post-Abrahamic OT history as well as of NT history. (For example, on page 60: "the basic historical character of Israel's monarchic period as described in the Old Testament cannot be seriously doubted.") If Enns's book was aimed at largely secular students of Scripture, I assume he would make a greater effort to affirm the basic historical character of the main biblical narratives. Yet in making his points about the basic historicity of biblical narratives, Enns follows central teachings of the NT itself (especially 1 Cor. 15:12-20 for the basic NT narrative of Christ's death and resurrection, and 1 Cor. 10:1-11 for the basic OT narrative of the exodus and following).[16] At the same time, he recognizes that standards of biblical history writing differ from modern standards of historical veracity, although he may not have specified how much different they are. And so he follows in a long line of distinguished theologians and biblical scholars — including Augustine, Calvin, James Orr, Ned Stonehouse, and N. T. Wright, among many others — by concluding that biblical assertions may not mean the same as modern assumptions would dictate when it comes to matters like chronology; numbers; the relationship between recorded single speeches (e.g., the Sermon on the Mount) and what was actually said in one or more speeches, or what reflected a broad set of teachings communicated in many different ways; the mingling of what moderns would consider myth into what they would consider verifiable

16. It is important that this second passage is one that Enns singles out for illustrating the power of Second Temple assumptions, especially concerning the rock that *followed* the Israelites. Thus, I think it would be Enns's position that the NT accepts the basic historicity of OT narratives, but that this acceptance is in terms of Second Temple hermeneutical usage, not modern historical proof.

history; and the absence of clear markers in history-type writing to distinguish among what we in recent centuries have come to differentiate as theological, ethical, and historical writing.

Finally, it is important to note that Enns's proposals do not contradict traditional affirmations about the inspiration, reliability, and authority of Scripture. To be sure, he does challenge many of the exegetical conclusions that believers in a high view of Scripture often take for granted, but not trust in Scripture itself.

*   *   *

The value that Christian scholars of all kinds can take away from Peter Enns's work does not lie primarily in the specifics of his conclusions. Rather, Enns allows scholars to realize afresh how crucial the Scriptures are for proclaiming Christ as redeemer and Lord, how important the Christ-centered message of Scripture is for understanding the Bible as a whole, and how basic the scriptural view of Christ is for all intellectual endeavors. Possessing a firm sense of what Scripture as a whole is about, approaching the Bible with greater critical self-consciousness about our own presuppositions and conventions of thought, and using the Bible (in life and in scholarship) more self-consciously and more thoroughly are the entirely positive purposes to which Enns's valuable book points.

If christological materials provide the right foundation for building other houses of learning, they offer the same for biblical study. Stressing the full humanity of divine revelation preserves believers from anti-intellectual gnosticism. Stressing the full divinity of revelation preserves believers from enervating secularism. Stressing the capacity of revelation to unite humanity and divinity in perfect integration puts believing scholars on the path to intellectual insight, but only because this is the path of life itself.

EIGHT

The Way Ahead

—◦◦◦—

It is important to underscore my intention for the preceding four chapters. The point is not to recruit scholars for particular programs or a specific set of conclusions about their disciplines (though I hope historians might read the history chapter as somewhat more than just rank naïveté). The much more pressing goal is to urge others into action. For "Christian scholarship" to mean anything, it must mean intellectual labor rooted in Christ, with both the rooting and the laboring essential. If even a few readers are moved to think about how their own scholarship might be connected organically to the great narratives summarized by the Christian creeds, or if only a few are spurred to pursue academic projects that draw self-consciously on their Christian faith, the effort will be worthwhile.

Yet action on such matters needs to be well-considered action. Especially in a day when doing something as soon as possible is the standard response to perceived problems, slowing down may be the best way to move ahead.

For matters relevant to believing scholars, the slowing down means realizing how basic Christianity must be for Christian scholarship. Life in Christ is a gift that makes all things new, including the vocations of learning, but it makes things new only because of how the gift is given and who the giver is. For rationale, means, methods, paradigms, and telos, the tasks of Christian scholarship depend pervasively on the work of God in Christ.

Believing scholars like myself who think that we have identified cultural or historical circumstances that impede responsible intellectual work can easily fall prey to a besetting temptation. The temptation is to think that if we have upbraided Christian communities for their anti-intellectual gnosticism, or if we have chastised the general academy for paying too little attention to Christian insights, we have somehow accomplished a great deal. In fact, even at their best, such criticisms or challenges are only like an official at a track meet calling competitors to the starting line.

Running the race is different. The race itself requires what the author of Hebrews calls throwing off hindrances and running with perseverance. But most of all it requires keeping the prize always in view: "Let us fix our eyes on Jesus, the author and perfecter of our faith, who for the joy set before him endured the cross, scorning its shame, and sat down at the right hand of the throne of God." For Christian life, including Christian academic life, to press on without growing weary and not losing heart, the scriptural injunction is simply to "consider him" (Heb. 12:2-3).

And so for scholarship that is Christian the essential ingredients are the same as for family life, politics, community service, economic activity, medical care, or any other activity that would be Christian. Those ingredients are prayer that returns to the source of forgiveness and hope, service that goes into the world in Christ's name, Bible reading or preaching or catechesis that rehearses the story of salvation, sacraments that instantiate the presence of Christ, fellowship that draws believers to each other and to their Lord, singing that inspires love of God and neighbor, sympathy that turns hearts toward the suffering, and meditation that draws the mind to God.

These essential ingredients of all Christian vocations rest upon the essential transaction that was framed memorably by Isaac Watts:

> See, from his head, his hands, his feet,
> sorrow and love flow mingled down.

Did e'er such love and sorrow meet,
or thorns compose so rich a crown?

Were the whole realm of nature mine,
that were an offering far too small;
love so amazing, so divine,
demands my soul, my life, my all.

The specific requirements for Christian scholarship all grow naturally from Christian worship inspired by such love: confidence in the ability to gain knowledge about the world because the world was brought into being through Jesus Christ; commitment to careful examination of the objects of study through "coming and seeing"; trust that good scholarship and faithful discipleship cannot ultimately conflict; humility from realizing that learning depends at every step on a merciful God; and gratitude in acknowledging that all good gifts come from above.

If, as Christians believe, "all the treasures of wisdom and knowledge" are hid in Christ (Col. 2:3), the time is always past for talking about treasure hunting. The time is always now to unearth treasure, offer it to others for critique or affirmation, and above all find in it new occasions to glorify the one who gives the treasure and is the treasure himself.

How Fares the "Evangelical Mind"?

——⟨ω/ω⟩——

N ow, early in the second decade of the twenty-first century, it is almost twenty years since I did the thinking and reading that went
into *The Scandal of the Evangelical Mind,* which was published in
1994.[1] About that book's historical arguments, its assessment of
evangelical strengths and weaknesses, and its indictment of evangelical intellectual efforts, I remain largely unrepentant. To be sure, the
perspective of time along with helpful comments from critics has
changed my mind on a few points. For instance, several readers were
right to complain that what I described as singularly evangelical problems were certainly related to the general intellectual difficulties of a
frenetic modern society. And it is certainly true that one of the reasons
that evangelicals do suffer from intellectual weakness is that American culture as a whole suffers from intellectual weakness. Another
criticism questioned the book's lumping together of fundamental-
ists, Pentecostals, and holiness advocates as culprits with neo-
evangelicals and dispensationalists more generally to explain the
downgrade of evangelical thinking. That criticism too was legitimate

---

1. This postscript is revised and expanded from "The Evangelical Mind Today,"
First Things, October 2004, 34-39, and "Christ-Centered Christian Learning," *Southern
Baptist Educator* 74, no. 4 (2003): 3-8.

since, in painting with a broad brush, the book did fail to recognize mitigating circumstances and telling exceptions in each of those subtraditions.

Yet on the whole, *The Scandal of the Evangelical Mind* still seems to me correct in its descriptions and evaluations. Like their compatriots throughout the world, Americans in pietistic, generically evangelical, Baptist, fundamentalist, Restorationist, Holiness, "Bible church," megachurch, or Pentecostal traditions face special difficulties when putting the mind to use. Taken together, American evangelicals display many virtues and do many things well, but built-in barriers to productive thinking remain substantial.

These barriers include an immediatism that insists on action, decision, and even perfection *right now;* a populism that confuses winning supporters with mastering actually existing situations; and an antitraditionalism that privileges current judgments on biblical, theological, and ethical issues (however hastily formed) over insight from the past (however hard won and carefully stated). In addition, as this book has suggested, we evangelicals are susceptible to a nearly gnostic dualism that rushes to spiritualize all manner of corporeal, terrestrial, physical, and material realities (despite the origin and providential maintenance of these realities by God). We also much prefer to put our money into programs offering immediate relief, whether evangelistic or humanitarian, instead of into institutions promoting intellectual development over the long term.

As a force in Christian history, evangelicalism has been a movement whose great strengths also define significant weaknesses. Compassionate concern for the immediate needs of individuals and their families, addressed right now, has been the defining trademark. Evangelicalism is a religion of conversion, and hence effective in proclaiming God's ability to change people immediately; it is a religion of revival, and hence committed to bringing life back into merely formal observance; it is a religion of the people, and hence able to recruit great numbers for meaningful Christian tasks. Yet these commendable traits pose problems for intellectual life, since serious thinking takes a lot of time, must honor the contributions of past generations, and often relies on the special insights of intellectual elites.

As a result, serious problems continue to bedevil evangelical thinking. We remain inordinately susceptible to enervating apocalyptic speculation, thus consuming oceans of bathetic end-times literature while sponsoring only a trickle of serious geopolitical analysis. We are consistently drawn to "American Christianities" — occasionally of the Left, more often of the Right — that subordinate principled reasoning rooted in the gospel to partisanship that demonizes opponents and excuses enormities in our friends. (Defense of the right to life remains the shining exception to political shallowness.) Progress has definitely been made at encouraging the arts and other creative endeavors, but capitulation to disembodied ideals of spirituality still hampers our struggling band of novelists and poets. And to repeat the judgments about science from chapter 6 above, far too many of us still make the intellectually suicidal mistake of promoting "creation science" as the best way to resist naturalistic philosophies of science. When it comes to the life of the mind, in other words, we evangelicals continue to have our problems.

At the same time, were I to attempt another full-scale historical assessment like *The Scandal of the Evangelical Mind,* it would have a different tone — more hopeful than despairing, more attuned to possibilities than to problems, more concerned with theological resources than with theological deficiencies. The major reason for this alteration is the argument set out in this book. Whatever may be the actual intellectual practice of Christian believers, the Christian faith contains all the resources, and more, required for full-scale intellectual engagement. And this engagement, as I have tried to argue, is fully compatible with the most basic beliefs and most essential practices of the faith.

To be sure, forces hostile to Christianity in the academy and in elite culture are large, vigorous, and growing rapidly. At some American universities and colleges, Christian scholars must operate as if from foxholes. In general, the intellectual climate is by no means propitious for Christian perspectives. No one can deny that in American society very strong trends are working against all intellectual efforts, and not just Christian efforts, to use the mind responsibly. These trends include, as a very partial list, the pace of modernity that has been accelerated by every one of the technological breakthroughs of recent decades; the nearly imbecile state of public political debate; the widespread striving for money and success as ends in themselves; the explosion of moral irresponsibility; and television.

Yet quite apart from what good theology should encourage and what contemporary culture often discourages, many developments in many evangelical domains do seem to be moving in the right direction. While some existed well before *The Scandal of the Evangelical Mind* was published, others have appeared more recently. This brief postscript cannot do justice to any of these developments, but a rapid catalogue may suggest that fairly substantial Christian thinking is now being carried out in many different ways throughout the landscape inhabited by North America's amorphous evangelical constituency.

Hopeful Signs

If there is great hope for intellectual life in the theology evangelicals profess to believe, so also can encouragement be found in at least ten developments of recent decades. How those developments should be ranked in importance is uncertain, but together they make an impressive list.

A first sign of hope comes from stirrings at evangelical colleges and universities. Because of how evangelicalism developed in the United States, evangelical institutions of higher learning have often functioned as sectarian enclaves; they have regularly sought purity in isolation over presence in public; and they have often been narrowly tied to the rise and fall of their dynamic leaders. These features have not necessarily been harmful for all Christian purposes, but for intellectual life they have been restricting. Over the last half century, however, more and more institutions of evangelical higher learning — colleges, universities, seminaries, and even Bible schools — have seasoned their sectarian certainties with commitment to "mere Christianity"; more and more have expanded goals beyond the socialization of their own group's rising generation; more and more have begun to promote the academic life as a legitimate Christian vocation; more and more are coming to understand that there can be no good teaching without good scholarship.

Evangelical higher education has been given a special boost in recent years by remarkable developments at Baylor University and by lower-key but still far-reaching initiatives at Calvin College. Baylor's characteristically Texan announcement that by the year 2012 it would dramatically improve the academic quality of its university and demonstrably raise the Christian salience of its academic programs met serious internal resistance. A predictable alliance of theological liberals and nervous naysayers protested, but many of Baylor's leading scholars forged ahead. With 2012 now at hand, it is clear that Baylor's grandest original goals have not been fully accomplished, but it is also clear that these efforts are continuing and that they constitute the most ambitious, far-reaching, and comprehensive institutional attempt in many decades to do the proper evangelical thing for the life of the mind.[2]

Calvin's special contribution to that same end has been its ambitious collection of summer seminars, organized for faculty and graduate students in a wide variety of fields and funded by several philanthropies (as well as by Calvin itself). These summer seminars, in place for more than a decade, provide instant networking for often isolated Christian scholars (and some who may not be Christian but want to engage with those who are). They offer opportunities for scholars from different Christian traditions to address important intellectual questions for the duration of a summer term and then through follow-up activities, and to do so at the level of a research university. The Calvin seminars are perhaps most intriguing as an experiment testing whether a college committed to solid undergraduate instruction can add promotion of serious research without taking on the whole of what has usually characterized America's comprehensive universities.

---

2. For perceptive midcourse evaluation, see Barry G. Hankins and Donald D. Schmeltekopf, eds., *The Baylor Project: Taking Christian Higher Education to the Next Level* (South Bend, IN: St. Augustine's, 2007).

In addition, a host of evangelical colleges — and also quasi-evangelical, evangelical-friendly, and evangelical fellow-traveling institutions — have started new programs, added faculty, set up institutes, sponsored conferences, raised money for research professorships, and otherwise taken steps to improve their intellectual quality. Many of these institutions are members of the Council of Christian Colleges and Universities, which from a Washington office has also worked hard to strengthen its members' intellectual efforts. Without having done a thorough investigation of such efforts, I am aware of significant steps undertaken at Biola, Eastern, George Fox, Gordon, Goshen, Indiana Wesleyan, Messiah, Ouachita, Patrick Henry, Pepperdine, Point Loma, Regent University, Samford, Seattle Pacific, Union, Valparaiso, Wheaton, Whitworth, Williams Baptist, and several Canadian institutions — Canadian Mennonite, Crandall (formerly Atlantic Baptist), King's, Redeemer, Regent, Trinity Western, and Tyndale. And doubtless much else is happening at other colleges as well. Evangelical higher education in North America remains a fragmented enterprise, both nourished and impeded by the sectarian character of American religion. But increasingly that kind of education is edging closer to serious sponsorship and lasting intellectual value.

A second reason for thinking more optimistically about evangelical intellectual life is the growing Christian presence at the nation's pluralistic universities, which enroll far more students of evangelical persuasion than do evangelical colleges and universities. One sign of that presence is a larger roster of identifiable Christian faculty in the lead ranks of their disciplines. Even though (or, perhaps, because) these visibly believing faculty take up their tasks in many different, not always compatible, ways, their very existence is a sign of hope. To compare today's situation with that in 1960 is to recognize a change for the better. While in 1960 there may have been a handful of leading scholars willing to identify themselves as believers, now it would be impossible to list all such scholars and their many fields of endeavor. Evangelicals who study with such individuals, read their works, or simply become aware of their existence are provided with examples of what they and their like might also do.

Other signs of hope at the pluralistic universities are modest but significant. Local churches and individual denominations maintain Christian study centers at many universities, and some of them are effective. Self-standing centers at Cornell, Illinois, Michigan, Michigan State, Minnesota, Virginia, and elsewhere offer encouragement by moving closer to the British and Canadian pattern where identifiably Christian units are embedded in the broader university. The newly formed Consortium of Christian Study Centers, whose director Drew Trotter had headed up the University of Virginia's effective study center, provides even more opportunities for these institutes to contribute than before. The Veritas Forums that annually convene on many campuses bring further connections, bibliographies, and encouragement to wide audiences that include many evangelicals.

At pluralistic colleges and universities, campus ministries of many sorts also encourage evangelical spiritual life, without which there would be no evangelical intellectual life. Especially with its major commitment to graduate and faculty ministry, InterVarsity Christian Fellowship has played an especially important role. By providing Christian nurture and networks for evangelical (and other) students and teachers who might otherwise feel isolated as believing scholars, the Grad-Faculty IVCF may be doing as much in its low-key way to improve evangelical intellectual life as any other ongoing national program. Such local efforts, which are sponsored by other campus ministries as well, are particularly important for enhancing networking, which is now absolutely essential for the contemporary tasks of Christian learning. In the relative absence of comprehensive evangelical universities, one can almost say that informal networks *are* the evangelical research universities.

A third hopeful sign is the maturity of evangelical theological seminaries. The traditional theological seminary may be hard pressed by many trends of recent years, including legitimate appeals for better preparation in practical ministries, declining salience of denominational traditions, megachurch sponsorship of on-site learning, and complicated requirements for second-career students. But the evangelical seminaries still excel as places of first-rate biblical scholarship, some encourage strong theology, and a few offer demanding Ph.D. programs that produce skillful scholars. In addition, the seminaries are the American evangelical institutions that have done the best job incorporating foreign students, with the enrichment brought by such students into their regular programs.

A fourth positive sign of hope is the growing cooperation between evangelical and Roman Catholic scholars that has contributed in several ways to improved evangelical use of the mind.[3] As more and more communication takes place between these once-warring camps, mutual enlightenment on many matters, including scholarship, is the result. So rapidly has the situation changed from the theological cold war that existed into the 1960s, it is now barely conceivable that either Catholics or evangelicals could once have thought that either could get along without help from the other. For Catholics, this exchange is probably more important for practical piety than for intellectual reasons, but the life of the mind is where evangelicals benefit most. While evangelicals offer Catholics eagerness, commitment, and know-how for negotiating in a culture of intellectual consumerism, Catholics offer evangelicals a sense of tradition, commitment, and centuries of reflection on the bearing of sacramentality for all existence.

Whenever evangelicals in recent years have been moved to admonish themselves and other evangelicals for weaknesses in ecclesiology, tradition, sacraments, theology of culture, aesthetics, philosophical theology, or historical consciousness, the result has almost always been selective appreciation for elements of the Catholic tradition. Whatever Protestants may think of individual proposals, methods, or conclusions proceeding from any individual Catholic thinker, the growing evangelical willingness to pay respectful attention to a whole host of Catholic intellectuals, beginning with the two most recent popes, John Paul II and Benedict XVI, makes an important contribution to better evangelical efforts.[4]

A fifth positive circumstance for evangelical scholarship is

3. For further discussion, see Mark A. Noll and James Turner, *The Future of Christian Learning: An Evangelical and Catholic Dialogue,* ed. Thomas Albert Howard (Grand Rapids: Brazos, 2008).

4. For an example of fruitful interchange, see Tim Perry, ed., *The Legacy of John Paul II: An Evangelical Assessment* (Downers Grove, IL: InterVarsity, 2007).

strong support from philanthropies. Savvy in finding and using this support has been one of the most important contributors to recent progress.[5] A number of foundations have done their part, including Fieldsted, Maclellan, Mustard Seed, Stewardship, and Templeton, but most notable have been the Lilly Endowment and the Pew Charitable Trusts. Under religious division directors Robert Lynn and Craig Dykstra, the Lilly Endowment has supported a number of evangelical enterprises as part of their effort to reinvigorate American religious life more generally.

Much of the substantial support for evangelical scholarship from the Pew Charitable Trusts passed through a variety of programs headquartered at the University of Notre Dame that flourished in the 1990s. These programs, with conceptual leadership provided by Nathan Hatch and implementation by Michael Hamilton, may have represented the most focused effort in all of American history to spur evangelicals to better Christian thinking. These ventures provided research fellowships for college and university professors, scholarships for graduate students, and seminars of various sorts for Christian academics at different stages of their careers.[6] Because the Notre Dame Pew programs deliberately kept definitions of "evangelical" flexible, they succeeded not only at encouraging substantial numbers of evangelicals, but also at establishing strong links with other Christians who were not evangelicals. The result was hundreds of students from evangelical colleges guided toward graduate education, scores of evangelical graduate students funded in leading doctoral programs, and dozens of older scholars assisted in finishing major writing projects.[7] In a word, the Pew initiatives at Notre Dame made evangelicals

5. That fund-raising savvy is treated perceptively in John A. Schmalzbauer, *People of Faith: Religious Conviction in American Journalism and Higher Education* (Ithaca, NY: Cornell University Press, 2003), and D. Michael Lindsay, *Faith in the Halls of Power: How Evangelicals Joined the American Elite* (New York: Oxford University Press, 2007).

6. For prospect and retrospect written, respectively, before and after the run of these programs, see Nathan O. Hatch, "Evangelical Colleges and the Challenge of Christian Thinking," *Reformed Journal,* September 1985, 10-18, and Michael S. Hamilton, "Patrons of the Evangelical Mind," *Christianity Today,* July 8, 2002, 42-47.

7. The remarkable range of major books supported by the Pew Programs included, among many others, C. Stephen Evans, *The Historical Christ and the Jesus of*

better scholars and also leveraged evangelical connections to improve Christian learning in general.

A sixth, more general arena has been the academic disciplines, with the ongoing renascence of Christian philosophy clearly leading the way. Beginning at midcentury with a few intrepid Calvinists and independent evangelicals, and stimulated by a large dose of modern Neo-Thomism, Christian philosophers have now for several decades been engaged in full-scale, first-order investigation at the highest level. Narrowly defined evangelicals have not dominated this Christian philosophical resurgence for which Roman Catholics, mainline Protestants, and representatives of historically ethnic churches were the leaders — like Robert Adams, William Alston, Alvin Plantinga, and Nicholas Wolterstorff. But card-carrying evangelicals, beginning with Arthur Holmes, who sponsored the first of Wheaton College's annual philosophy conferences in 1954, and Asbury College with its noteworthy support for philosophical organizations, have been key participants at every stage. For evangelical graduate students and young professionals, philosophy has become the one academic discipline where strong networks devoted to both intellectual rigor and Christian integrity exist in all regions of the country and for almost every level of higher education.

Results of this resurgence are visible in the quality of work being produced, where, for example, philosophers and theologians attuned to modern philosophy provide an unusually high proportion of the serious orthodox theology on offer in the English-speaking world. The Society of Christian Philosophers, founded in 1978, sponsors a highly regarded journal, *Faith and Philosophy,* that is edited by a distin-

---

Faith (New York: Oxford University Press, 1996); Richard Hays, *The Moral Vision of the New Testament* (San Francisco: HarperSanFrancisco, 1996); E. Brooks Holifield, *Theology in America* (New Haven: Yale University Press, 2003); Roger Lundin, *Emily Dickinson and the Art of Belief* (Grand Rapids: Eerdmans, 1996); Lamin Sanneh, *Encountering the West* (Maryknoll, NY: Orbis, 1993); Dale Van Kley, *The Religious Origins of the French Revolution* (New Haven: Yale University Press, 1996); Geoffrey Wainwright, *Lesslie Newbigin: A Theological Life* (New York: Oxford University Press, 2000); and Nicholas Wolterstorff, *Divine Discourse: Philosophical Reflections on the Claim That God Speaks* (New York: Cambridge University Press, 1995).

guished body of stellar scholars and sponsored by a mixture of Catholic, evangelical, and mainline Protestant institutions. For evangelicals, the continuing strength of the Christian philosophy project has provided stimulus, encouragement, models, graduate school mentors, practice in intra-Christian diversity, and much more. Other academic disciplines — including history, the visual arts, economics, political science, sociology, music, law, and the physical sciences — enjoy active Christian networks, but none has reached as high or mixed as many Christian traditions so productively as the Christian philosophers.[8] No other academic network has contributed so directly to the strengthening of evangelical minds.

A seventh mark of at least some progress is the domain of science. In the past, warfare over evolution may have been necessary, especially to protect students from crude philosophical naturalism masquerading as empirical science. But it was also regrettable, especially by transforming questions requiring measured and learned investigation into public arguments favoring simplistic demagoguery by theists and secularists alike. Strife over "creation science" continues to meander along, and so continues to exact a high cost in both serious study of nature and serious learning from Scripture. But as suggested in this book (chapter 6), efforts on many fronts are moving discussions to new levels of seriousness. Professional organizations like the American Scientific Affiliation, which publishes a wide-ranging journal, *Perspectives on Science and Christian Faith,* have long pointed the way to more responsible attention to a broad range of sciences. Some leaders of the Intelligent Design movement have pushed discussions to first-order questions of metaphysics and teleology where discussion should have been focusing all along. And newer ventures like the BioLogos Founda-

8. For an account featuring the pioneering work among historians of the Nazarene scholar Timothy L. Smith and the Reformed scholar George Marsden (who in 2004 won the Bancroft Prize, the nation's most distinguished award in historical writing, for his biography of Jonathan Edwards), see Mark A. Noll, "How an Evangelical Won the Bancroft Prize: Lessons for Christian Scholars from the Recent History of One Discipline," in *American Evangelicalism: George Marsden and the Shape of American Religious History,* ed. Kurt W. Peterson, Thomas S. Kidd, and Darren Dochuk (forthcoming).

tion are trying to show that commitment to traditional Christianity does not equal scientific obscurantism.

An eighth arena where favorable developments have helped evangelicals toward greater intellectual responsibility is the world of publishing. Serious periodicals like *Books & Culture, Commonweal, First Things, Image,* and *Touchstone* provide meaningful engagement with significant issues of contemporary life. Whether such journals do so from explicitly evangelical angles or from the perspective of other believing traditions, their net effect is to demonstrate how essential it is for communities of faith to think their way through — as well as just reacting to — the modern world.

The number of serious books that can be identified as Christian, near-Christian, or Christian-friendly also continues to expand. Firms like Eerdmans, Baker, and InterVarsity Press, who were midwives at the birth of postwar evangelicalism, have continued to perform Herculean labors. But they have also been joined by many other religious, commercial, and university presses that are willing to publish books by evangelicals or that treat seriously the subjects that most concern evangelicals.

Developments in world Christianity constitute a ninth reason for hope. Together, North American Catholics and evangelicals share the privilege of many contacts with their fellow believers in the Two-Thirds World, where Christian expansion and Christian creativity — if also, Christian confusion — are beginning to impinge on Western consciousness. The dimensions and implications of the new world Christianity have been well documented in important studies by a growing number of scholars, including Andrew Walls, Lamin Sanneh, Dana Robert, David Martin, and Philip Jenkins. Christian links between the First World and the Two-Thirds World have especially great potential benefits for scholarship.[9] Those links remind Westerners about what an unusual privilege it is to have the time, money, and health for academic tasks. They help display the power of the Christian gospel afresh. They teach much about the importance of suffer-

---

9. See especially Joel A. Carpenter, "Christian Higher Education as a Worldwide Movement," *Journal of Latin American Theology* 3 (2008): 71-98.

ing for Christian discipleship. They can work against many of the evils that bedevil Western intellectual life (narcissism, colonialism, unthinking individualism). And they offer many new partners for exploring the full range of academic questions and academic disciplines. If Andrew Walls is right — that the historic advances in clarifying Christian doctrines have always occurred in situations where the faith is being transmitted cross-culturally — then we should expect as well that profound Christian insight is going to come to us from the Two-Thirds World, and that this insight could be a tremendous spur to creative Christian thinking in the West.[10]

A last reason for modest optimism about Christian learning in contemporary North America stems from an awareness of the positive effect that individual Christian scholars are having in the broader academy. Whether in guiding major publication projects like the *Works of Jonathan Edwards,* speaking out as younger African American scholars about traditional religious concerns, defending Christian orthodoxy in departments of English, or leading as teachers or researchers in numerous venues, individuals continue to make a difference. One example of a scholar who passed away in 1995 can serve as representative of a much greater number.

George Rawlyk, who for many years had been a major presence as professor and sometime chair of history at Queen's University, Kingston, Ontario, illustrated the difference an individual could make. Through a series of circumstances in the early 1980s Rawlyk became a strong supporter of Wheaton College's Institute for the Study of American Evangelicals and a moving force in many of its projects. A giant of a man in every sense of the word, Rawlyk, the son of Ukrainian immigrants, gave up prospects for a career in Canadian pro football to take a Rhodes scholarship at Oxford and to pursue an academic career. The research interests he cultivated through a score or more of books included the early history of the Maritime Provinces, the story of evangelicalism throughout Canadian history, and the relation of religion

---

10. Andrew F. Walls, *The Missionary Movement in Christian History* (Maryknoll, NY: Orbis, 1996), and *The Cross-Cultural Process in Christian History* (Maryknoll, NY: Orbis, 2002).

and Canadian politics.[11] He mentored the authors of more than one hundred master's theses and doctoral dissertations and provided an incredible range of support — intellectual, financial, and emotional — to many more students, colleagues, and friends. In a combination that has not been common on the American side of the border, George's life-direction was set in his teens by influential contact with labor radicalism and Baptist evangelicalism. Throughout his adult life he was an ardent supporter of the New Democratic Party, Canada's socialist alternative to the Liberals and Conservatives, and he also regularly sponsored InterVarsity and other student Christian groups. He was an active Baptist layman and often served as a deacon at his Kingston church. Yet throughout the first part of his career, Rawlyk struggled to unite his vocations as historian, socialist, and evangelical. When from about 1980, however, he began to read the historical works of George Marsden, he saw how it might be possible to bring together personal faith and historical research. To be sure, the way Rawlyk united the spheres of his life was unique — on historical as well as political matters, he called no man master. But the relief he expressed at finding a body of American historians who tried to bring faith and scholarship together energized him remarkably. In turn, his sanctified Slavic empathy made him a great encouragement to many of us colder Teutonic types in the United States, as well as in Canada.

The reality obvious at Rawlyk's funeral, through several memorial services, and in the years following his death was that a very broad circle had been touched by this one life. That circle included evangelicals, mainline Protestants, Roman Catholics, and many who professed no faith. But all agreed that Rawlyk had given strong legitimization to the serious study of Canadian religious history, even in the recent past when Canada was secularizing much more rapidly than the United States. With a rare combination of intellectual integrity, personal integrity, and religious integrity, Rawlyk touched many scholars and showed all who were willing to see what such integrity could mean.

---

11. For an accounting, see P. L. Coops and D. J. Hessler, "George Alexander Rawlyk: A Bibliography, 1962-1996," *Acadiensis: Journal of the History of the Atlantic Region* 26 (1997): 159-73.

Christian Scholarship by Evangelicals
More Than Evangelical Christian Scholarship

Evangelical intellectual life is being strengthened by developments in each of these areas and probably more that could be mentioned. Yet when assessing the current situation, realism is also required. We are indeed witnessing improvement in Christian intellectual life from evangelicals, but this improvement does not point toward the development of a distinctly evangelical mind. Common, generic evangelicalism, as also the activistic denominations and strong parachurch agencies that dominate the movement as a whole, does not possess theologies full enough, traditions of intellectual practice strong enough, or conceptions of the world deep enough to sustain a full-scale intellectual revival.

Without strong theological traditions, many evangelicals lack a critical element required for making intellectual activity both self-confident and properly humble, both critical and committed. To advance responsible Christian learning, the vitality of commitment needs the ballast of tradition. If evangelicals are well aware that tradition without life is a serious problem, they are less conscious that life without tradition presents its own difficulties.

Part of what makes it possible for a particular stream of Christianity to support vigorous intellectual life is simply the passage of time. Older movements have had more opportunities to broaden out into fruitful scholarship. But part is also a self-conscious commitment to learn from the teaching and experience of past believing generations. The current dilemma for Christian learning in North America could be described, though too simplistically, in the following generalizations. On the one side, Pentecostals, Southern Baptists, members of Holiness movements, seeker-sensitive churches, dispensationalists, Adventists, African American congregations, radical Wesleyans, and lowest-common-denominator evangelicals have great spiritual energy, but flounder in putting the mind to use for Christ. On the other hand, Lutherans, Catholics, Anglo-Catholics, the Reformed, and even the Eastern Orthodox enjoy incredibly rich traditions that include sterling examples of Christian thought, but often display a comatose spirituality.

This picture is, of course, an exaggeration. Yet think how easy it is to talk about Pentecostal signs and wonders, intense Holiness spirituality, vigorous seeker-sensitive evangelism, a dispensationalist devotion to Scripture, and Baptist missionary zeal. It is almost as easy to discover an estimable tradition of Lutheran sacred music, art history pursued from a Kuyperian Reformed perspective, profound social theory from Catholics, and a solid trajectory of Anglo-Catholic *belles lettres.* But then shift the categories and hear how strange it sounds: Kuyperian Reformed signs and wonders? Vigorous Catholic evangelism? An Anglo-Catholic devotion to Scripture? Intense Lutheran spirituality? Or, to do it the other way: An estimable tradition of Holiness sacred music? Art history pursued from a Baptist perspective? A solid trajectory of seeker-sensitive *belles lettres?* Profound social theory from the Holiness movement?

Active Christian life of the sort that defines evangelicalism is a prerequisite for responsible Christian learning. But unless that activity is given shape, it will not be particularly effective. The shape that the older Christian traditions provide is deep, because they are rooted in classical Christian doctrine, and it is wide, because they have nurtured outstanding examples of faithful Christian thinking. There is, in other words, no Neo-Thomist personalism in philosophy without centuries of God-honoring moral casuistry, no J. S. Bach without Luther's theologies of the incarnation and the cross, no Dorothy L. Sayers without Anglo-Catholic sacramentalism, no Flannery O'Connor without a Catholic theology of redemption, and no contemporary revival of Christian philosophy among American evangelicals without the legacy of Kuyperian Calvinism.

Evangelicals of several types are beginning to learn the lessons taught by such exemplars. As they do, many are becoming more serious Christian thinkers. To embrace the energy of American evangelicalism, but also to move beyond the eccentricities of American evangelicalism into the spacious domains of self-critical, patient, rooted, and productive Christian reflection, remains the great challenge for evangelicals eager to serve Christ with the mind.

The goals in view can be simply stated:

- to promote careful study of Scripture that stresses the life-altering glories of Jesus Christ, rather than the whims of private eurekas;
- to promote thoughtful Christian reflection that comes from theology based on the whole of Scripture and infused with insights from Christian tradition, rather than marred by sloganeering and proof texting;
- to promote thoughtful approaches to the problems of life that are heavy on analysis but light on ideology and simplification;
- to promote effective communication in forms appropriate for both Christian communities and modern pluralistic culture, instead of resorting to demagoguery and mindless grandstanding; and
- to promote broad engagement with the world that includes knowledgeable awareness of science, balanced approaches to politics, and active support for the arts, instead of reacting with fear and suspicion to the enterprises of intellectual culture.

To steal Charles Dickens's oft-borrowed line: when considering all the impediments that evangelicals bring to intellectual life, one can conclude that it must be the worst of times; but when considering positive developments in recent decades, and even more the unmatched treasures in Jesus Christ, one might conclude that it is also the best of times.

Further Reading

———❧❧❧———

This bibliography has two sections. The first lists the kinds of books that I read or sampled in trying to obtain a firmer grasp of Christology. The second contains helpful material on different aspects of Christian learning that has been published since 1994 when *The Scandal of the Evangelical Mind* appeared. It goes without saying that even reasonably adequate treatment of especially the first topic would require a much, much larger bibliography.

Christology

Balthasar, Hans Urs von. *Mysterium Paschale: The Mystery of Easter.* San Francisco: Ignatius, 1990.

Blocher, Henri. *La Doctrine du Christ.* Vaux-sur-Seine, France: Edifac, 2002.

Bloesch, Donald G. *Jesus Christ: Savior and Lord.* Downers Grove, IL: InterVarsity, 1997.

Boersma, Hans. *Violence, Hospitality, and the Cross: Reappropriating the Atonement Tradition.* Grand Rapids: Baker, 2004.

Elliott, Mark, and John L. McPake, eds. *The Only Hope: Jesus Yesterday, Today, Forever.* Fearn, Ross-shire, Scotland: Christian Focus, 2001.

Horton, Michael. *Lord and Servant: A Covenant Christology.* Louisville: Westminster John Knox, 2005.

McGrath, Alister E. *Luther's Theology of the Cross.* Oxford: Blackwell, 1985.

Marshall, I. Howard. *I Believe in the Historical Jesus.* Grand Rapids: Eerdmans, 1977.

Neuhaus, Richard John. *Death on a Friday Afternoon: Meditations on the Last Words of Jesus from the Cross.* New York: Basic Books, 2000.

Piper, John. *The Passion of Jesus Christ.* Wheaton, IL: Crossway, 2004.

Seitz, Christopher R., ed. *Nicene Christianity: The Future for a New Ecumenism.* Grand Rapids: Brazos, 2001.

Steinmetz, David C. *Luther in Context.* Grand Rapids: Baker, 1995.

Stott, John R. W. *The Cross of Christ.* Downers Grove, IL: InterVarsity, 1986.

———. *The Incomparable Christ.* Downers Grove, IL: InterVarsity, 2001.

Webster, John. "Jesus Christ." In *The Cambridge Companion to Evangelical Theology,* edited by Timothy Larsen and Daniel J. Treier. New York: Cambridge University Press, 2007.

Wells, David F. *The Person of Christ: A Biblical and Historical Analysis of the Incarnation.* Westchester, IL: Crossway, 1984.

Wright, N. T. *The Challenge of Jesus: Rediscovering Who Jesus Was and Is.* Downers Grove, IL: InterVarsity, 1999.

Christian Scholarship

Barron, Robert. *The Priority of Christ: Toward a Postliberal Catholicism.* Grand Rapids: Brazos, 2007.

Benne, Robert. *Quality with Soul: How Six Premier Christian Colleges and Universities Keep Faith with Their Religious Traditions.* Grand Rapids: Eerdmans, 2001.

Berger, Peter L., ed. *Between Relativism and Fundamentalism: Religious Resources for a Middle Position.* Grand Rapids: Eerdmans, 2010.

Burtchaell, James T. *The Dying of the Light: The Disengagement of Colleges and Universities from Their Christian Churches.* Grand Rapids: Eerdmans, 1998.

Cherry, Conrad, Betty DeBerg, and Amanda Porterfield. *Religion on Campus.* Chapel Hill: University of North Carolina Press, 2001.

Craig, William Lane, and Paul M. Gould, eds. *The Two Tasks of the Christian Scholar: Redeeming the Soul, Redeeming the Mind.* Wheaton, IL: Crossway, 2007.

Crouch, Andy. *Culture Making: Recovering Our Christian Calling.* Downers Grove, IL: InterVarsity, 2008.

Curry, Janel M., and Ronald A. Wells, eds. *Faithful Imagination in the Academy.* Lanham, MD: Lexington, 2008.

Franklin, Patrick. "Teaching, Scholarship, and Christian Worldview: A Review of Recent Literature." *McMaster Journal of Theology and Ministry* 11 (2009-10): 28-61.

Gleason, Philip. *Contending with Modernity: Catholic Higher Education in the Twentieth Century.* New York: Oxford University Press, 1995.

Gregory, Brad. "No Room for God? History, Science, Metaphysics, and the Study of Religion." *History and Theory* 47 (2008): 495-519.

Guinness, Os. *Fit Bodies, Fat Minds: Why Evangelicals Don't Think and What to Do about It.* Grand Rapids: Baker, 1994.

Hart, D. G. *The University Gets Religion: Religious Studies in American Higher Education.* Baltimore: Johns Hopkins University Press, 1999.

Hauerwas, Stanley. *The State of the University: Academic Knowledge and the Knowledge of God.* Oxford: Wiley-Blackwell, 2007.

Heie, Harold, and Michael A. King, eds. *Mutual Treasure: Seeking Better Ways for Christians and Culture to Converse.* Telford, PA: Cascadia, 2009.

Henry, Douglas V., and Michael D. Beaty, eds. *Christianity and the Soul of the University: Faith as a Foundation for Intellectual Community.* Grand Rapids: Baker, 2006.

Holmes, Arthur. *The Soul of the Christian University.* Stob Lectures, 1996-97. Grand Rapids: Calvin College, 1997.

Hughes, Richard. *How Christian Faith Can Sustain the Life of the Mind.* Grand Rapids: Eerdmans, 2001.

Hughes, Richard, and William B. Adrian, eds. *Models for Christian Higher Education: Strategies for Success in the Twenty-First Century.* Grand Rapids: Eerdmans, 1997.

Hull, William E. *The Quest for Spiritual Maturity.* Dotson M. Nelson Jr. Lecture, 2002. Birmingham, AL: Samford University, 2004.

Hunter, James Davison. *To Change the World: The Irony, Tragedy, and Possibility of Christianity in the Late Modern World.* New York: Oxford University Press, 2010.

Jacobsen, Douglas, and Rhonda Hustedt Jacobsen, eds. *The American University in a Postsecular Age.* New York: Oxford University Press, 2008.

Lindsay, D. Michael. *Evangelicals in the Halls of Power: How Evangelicals Joined the American Elite.* New York: Oxford University Press, 2007.

Litfin, A. Duane. *Conceiving the Christian College.* Grand Rapids: Eerdmans, 2004.

MacIntyre, Alasdair. *God, Philosophy, Universities: A Selective History of the Catholic Philosophical Tradition.* Lanham, MD: Rowman and Littlefield, 2009.

Marsden, George M. *The Outrageous Idea of Christian Scholarship.* New York: Oxford University Press, 1997.

———. *The Soul of the American University: From Protestant Establishment to Established Nonbelief.* New York: Oxford University Press, 1994.

Moreland, J. P. *Love God with All Your Mind: The Role of Reason in the Life of the Soul.* Colorado Springs: NavPress, 1997.

Morey, Melanie M., and John J. Piderit, S.J. *Catholic Higher Education: A Culture in Crisis.* New York: Oxford University Press, 2006.

Mouw, Richard J. *He Shines in All That's Fair: Culture and Common Grace.* Grand Rapids: Eerdmans, 2001.

Noll, Mark A., and James Turner. *The Future of Christian Learning.* Edited by Thomas Albert Howard. Grand Rapids: Brazos, 2008.

Piper, John. *Think: The Life of the Mind and the Love of God.* Wheaton, IL: Crossway, 2010.

Schmalzbauer, John A. *People of Faith: Conviction in American Journalism and Higher Education.* Ithaca, NY: Cornell University Press, 2003.

Sire, James W. *Habits of the Mind: Intellectual Life as a Christian Calling.* Downers Grove, IL: InterVarsity, 2000.

Skeel, David A., Jr. "The Paths of Christian Legal Scholarship." *The Green Bag: An Entertaining Journal of Law* 12 (Winter 2009): 169-83.

Sommerville, C. John. *The Decline of the Secular University.* New York: Oxford University Press, 2006.

———. *Religious Ideas for Secular Universities.* Grand Rapids: Eerdmans, 2009.

Taylor, Charles. *A Catholic Modernity?* Edited by James L. Heft (with responses by William M. Shea, Rosemary Luling Haughton, George Marsden, and Jean Bethke Elshtain). New York: Oxford University Press, 1999.

Veith, Gene Edward, Jr. *Loving God with All Your Mind: Thinking as a Christian in the Postmodern World.* Rev. ed. Wheaton, IL: Crossway, 2003.

Wainwright, William J., ed. *God, Philosophy, and Academic Culture.* Atlanta: Scholars, 1996.

Wells, Ronald A., ed. *Keeping Faith: Embracing the Tensions in Christian Higher Education.* Grand Rapids: Eerdmans, 1996.

Williams, Clifford. *The Life of the Mind: A Christian Perspective.* Grand Rapids: Baker, 2002.

Acknowledgments

—⟨ɔʃɔ⟩—

I am grateful first for those who responded to *The Scandal of the Evangelical Mind* by asking me to lecture at their institutions or to their organizations about the subjects of that book. They are the ones most responsible for this effort at fleshing out the very sketchy remarks about a positive approach to Christian learning that appeared in the last chapter of that earlier volume. The generosity, hospitality, and intellectual stimulation I received from these groups were invariably greater than what I could communicate to them.

At Wheaton College I was privileged on three occasions to lead faculty seminars on the subject of Christology and scholarship. The oversight of Provost Stan Jones and the insights of all who participated in these seminars were a great gift; I only hope that I have not smuggled too many of my colleagues' ideas into this book as if they were my own. In a larger sense, *Jesus Christ and the Life of the Mind* tries to describe the extraordinary resources for intellectual life latent in the evangelical Protestant tradition that Wheaton represents, and for which I remain profoundly grateful. Since, however, I have also benefited more recently from approaches to Christian learning pursued at the University of Notre Dame, I am pleased to thank my new colleagues, and especially Brad Gregory, for the Catholic leavening they have generously supplied to my evangelical perspective.

Acknowledgments

I am aware of special indebtedness to Nathan Hatch, George Marsden, David Wells, Neal Plantinga, and the late George Rawlyk who many years ago initiated the project that has led to this second book on the theme of Christian learning, and to four other individuals for unusual assistance: to John Wilson for making *Books & Culture* into such a lively demonstration of Christian learning at work; to David Livingstone for communicating so much wisdom while waiting so patiently for the last lecture to be written for our course, "Christianity and Science: From Copernicus to the Creationists and Beyond"; to Roger Lundin for showing so ably in person and in print how fruits may be harvested from seemingly barren soil; and to Bruce Kuklick for being so skeptical about this entire project and so helpful in how he expressed that skepticism. At the risk of forgetting others who provided unusual help during the long germination of this book, I would also like to offer a particular word of thanks to David Bebbington, Joel Carpenter, Helen DeVries, Mike Hamilton, Darryl Hart, Bob and JoAnne Harvey, David Hempton, Arthur Holmes, Mark Hutchinson, Alan Jacobs, the late Ogbu Kalu, Tom Kay, Duane Litfin, Kathryn Long, John McGreevy, Jim Moore, Tom Noble, John Piper, Joel Sheesley, John Stackhouse, Grant Wacker, and John Walford. I am especially grateful for helpful suggestions from Craig Noll and for expert editing from Tom Raabe.

With every bit of writing that appears under my name, I am more and more conscious of the coauthorship that belongs by rights to Maggie Noll. She has been and continues to be sine qua non.

The book's dedication offers sincerest thanks to an editor of extraordinary patience and by extension to the extraordinary publishing company that employs him, which for now a full century has been promoting the goals outlined in this book.

Index of Names and Subjects

—◆◇◆—

Index of Scripture References

—⁓⁓—

INDEX OF SCRIPTURE REFERENCES